CANADA'S
WAR GROOMS
AND THE GIRLS
Who Stole Their Hearts

BY JUDY KOZAR

Published by

GENERAL STORE
PUBLISHING HOUSE

499 O'Brien Rd., Box 415
Renfrew, Ontario, Canada K7V 4A6
Telephone (613) 432-7697 or 1-800-465-6072
www.gsph.com

ISBN 978-1-897113-69-1
Printed and Bound in Canada

Cover design and formatting by Robyn Hader
Printing by Custom Printers of Renfrew Ltd.

Library and Archives Canada Cataloguing in Publication

Kozar, Judy, 1943-
    Canada's war grooms and the girls who stole their hearts / Judy Kozar.

ISBN 978-1-897113-69-1

    1. War grooms--Canada--Biography. 2. Soldiers--Commonwealth
countries--Biography. 3. World War, 1939-1945--Canada. 4. World War,
1939-1945--Personal narratives. I. Title.

D811.A2K69 2007   940.54'81   C2007-902452-1

This book is dedicated to Bill Thomas,
my stepfather-in-law, who
unwittingly provided the inspiration.

Note to Readers

This book is not intended to be a historical document, but rather a collection of memories of the men and women who "were there." Memories, however, are not perfect, and there may be an occasional error or omission. For this we apologize, but take no responsibility.

TABLE OF CONTENTS

INTRODUCTION

Not another war book! Bookshelves groan under the weight of countless memoirs written by participants who "were there" as events unfolded during World War II. Yet, the number of war books continues to grow as war babies and baby boomers, including myself, write still more accounts about those participants. Who would have thought that there are still more untold stories that took place during one of the darkest periods of human history? Well, the war groom story is an unexplored part of Canada's military past, and it is time that these men receive the attention due them.

Although almost every one knows or knows of a war bride, many people have never heard of war grooms. Well, they do exist, and their stories exemplify true romance, dedication to duty, and lives well lived. But who are they? In short, they are the male counterparts of the war brides. For the purpose of this book, war grooms are non-Canadian, Allied servicemen who met Canadian girls during World War II, married them during or after the war, and emigrated to Canada as a result of the relationship.

My stepfather-in-law, Bill Thomas, was a war groom. He was a quiet, introspective man who never talked much about his war experiences. I was positive there was a side to him that he chose not to reveal, but I knew he would not allow anyone to delve into those recesses. I did know, however, that he came from Britain to be trained as a pilot in Canada during the war, and that he married a Canadian girl while he was here, although that marriage was not successful.

Bill and my widowed mother-in-law met, fell in love, and married when they were both in their seventies. I recall my husband's reaction when he first learned that Bill was seriously courting his mother. Being very protective, he wanted to find out if Bill's intentions were honourable. Needless to say, they were, and Bill was warmly welcomed into our family. My daughters, who were teenagers at the time, were both intrigued and amused when they first learned that their grandmother was dating.

After Bill died on February 25, 2005, we found his brief memoirs among his papers, and his story fascinated me. I felt that there had to be other war grooms in Canada with similar experiences, and as far as I could tell, no one had dealt with this aspect of our military history. I have enjoyed reading the accounts of war brides over the years, and I knew that the war groom stories would be equally as compelling.

My goals were (1) to document the stories of these men and the Canadian girls who stole their hearts before it was too late; and (2) to emphasize the tremendous effort it took to win the war. I then embarked upon a journey that consumed me for many months.

At this point, I should say something about my journey. I started by contacting the Western Canada Aviation Museum in Winnipeg and was given the names of a few war grooms in the area. My first shot in the dark proved to be fruitful, and I was encouraged. I then contacted a friend who grew up in Carberry, Manitoba, the site of a wartime service training flying school. She gave me the names of a few of the local girls who married RAF servicemen and placed an advertisement on my behalf in the Carberry and Neepawa newspapers. I wanted to include war grooms from across Canada, however, and in order to do this, I had to have national coverage. Several historical societies, military and aviation museums, and war bride associations were very helpful and agreed to advertise my project in their newsletters and on their web sites. The Wartime Pilots' and Observers' Association, *The Legion Magazine, Airforce Magazine*, Friends of the Canadian War Museum, The Army, Navy, and Airforce Veterans in Canada, and 1 Canadian Air Division Headquarters were also very helpful. Elizabeth Lapointe, a freelance journalist, interviewed me, and wrote an article about war grooms in *The Maple Leaf*, a newspaper for the Canadian military.

Many contacts came through referrals as a result of all the coverage. There were a few war grooms who chose not to be included, some because of ill health and others for reasons they chose not to disclose. In one case, I got the impression that the war groom's second wife was somewhat jealous of the deceased first wife. Occasionally, I reached a dead end when I discovered that both the war groom and his wife had passed away. Sometimes, the surviving relatives, even when I did manage to find them, didn't know enough to generate a story. I began to think that maybe I was ten years too late in trying to write a book of this nature. The stories continued to trickle in, however, and I plodded on.

After I made contact with war grooms, their widows, or children, I explained my purpose and gave them a list of questions, but I emphasized that it was the "love story" that interested me the most. Some of the stories were written by the war grooms, their widows or children. Other stories were written after interviews were conducted. In the cases of Bob Kellow and Bob Metcalfe, who are both deceased, I wrote summaries based on their published autobiographies, supplemented with other details submitted by members of their families. Kenneth McDonald sent me a copy of his published autobiography, *A Wind on the Heath: a Memoir*, and I used his words wherever possible when crafting his story. I have signed consent and waiver forms from all contributors.

The war grooms in this book are probably a fairly accurate representation of the entire group, but it is difficult to tell because of the lack of documentation. During the war, the war grooms in this book served in many different capacities and were posted throughout the world. After emigration, they resided, literally, in communities stretching from coast to coast.

Several books have been written about the war brides over the years, and their stories have given us many hours of interesting reading. War grooms provide fascinating reading, too, not only because of their love stories, but also because of their war experiences. Their military careers were stellar! I am positive there are many more fascinating stories of war grooms waiting to be told. Perhaps a sequel? Who knows?

Future historians might want to document the stories of the Canadian girls who went to live abroad permanently after they married non-Canadian servicemen. It might also be interesting to find out if any Canadian girls married German POWs who were interned in Canada during the war. Yes, there are even more untold stories to be written. It is fortunate that many of us have an insatiable appetite for personal accounts about World War II.

War brides have received a great deal of media attention in recent years, and deservedly so. Their stories have often been related on television and in print. Since the Canadian government provided passage for most of these women and their children, documentation exists. As a result of marriages between Canadian servicemen and girls from other countries, Canada welcomed 48,000 war brides and 22,000 children to its shores.[1] The war brides continued to add to their families after emigration. The number of children, grandchildren and great-grandchildren descended from war brides must now be in the hundreds of thousands.

Conversely, I could find no documentation on war grooms. Because they weren't Canadian servicemen, Veterans Affairs has no record of them. To this day, we have no idea how many of them there were.

Many of the war grooms came to Canada because of the British Commonwealth Air Training Plan (BCATP). From October 1940 to March 1945, aircrew from various countries became BCATP graduates: 42,110 from Britain, 9,606 from Australia, and 7,002 from New Zealand.[2] These numbers do not include the 5,296 Royal Air Force personnel who were trained here before the BCATP came into effect.

[1] Linda Granfield, *Brass Buttons and Silver Horseshoes* (Toronto: McClelland & Stewart Ltd., 2002), p. 2.

[2] Spencer Dunmore, *Wings for Victory* (Toronto: McClelland & Stewart Inc., 1994), p. 361.

In addition, the numbers do not include servicemen from countries other than the U.K., Australia or New Zealand, those graduating from groundcrew schools, or the many thousands of airmen who helped to operate the training schools. Because of the BCATP, there were thousands of eligible young airmen with interesting accents in Canada during the war, and it was inevitable that they would meet and marry Canadian girls.

Most of the war grooms in this book were airmen, with four exceptions. One was in the British army, and three others were sailors (Royal Navy and the Norwegian merchant navy). There were fewer opportunities for servicemen from these two branches to meet Canadian girls during the war.

The Second World War was a cataclysmic event, and it changed the lives of millions of people. It certainly shook up the world's gene pool. It was an intense time, and one tended to live for the moment with no thought of tomorrow. This mindset may have been a factor in some of the hasty wartime marriages that occurred. In some cases, the couples married after brief, whirlwind courtships. "It will never last!" was a common refrain from family and friends. The engaged couples, some of them still in their teens, could not be dissuaded. After viewing the wedding pictures that were submitted, I know why Canadian girls fell head over heels in love with these handsome, dashing young men in uniform.

In most cases, the war grooms did not experience the same degree of culture shock after emigration that the war brides did. With the exception of Bob Metcalfe, all of the war grooms in this book had been to Canada before they married. They had experienced the climate and knew something of the customs and culture. They were impressed with what they saw and experienced in this country before they married and moved here.

The war grooms still talk about the hospitality of Canadians during the war. Families opened their homes and hearts to the lonely young servicemen, most of whom were away from home for the first time. The young men, many hardly more than growing boys, were always hungry, and Canadians made sure they were well fed. The servicemen from countries with shortages of almost everything appreciated the bounty from Canadian kitchens. Communities also provided entertainment for the boys in uniform, particularly dances where many a war groom met his future wife.

Some of the war grooms I interviewed were surprised that anyone would want to document their war experiences or love stories. One gentleman said, "Who would want to read that stuff?" Well, everyone enjoys a good love story. Some of the war grooms in this book passed away before I even began my research. Their widows and children happily provided the information and were pleased that their husbands and fathers were finally being recognized.

The hand-written letter, disparagingly referred to these days as "snail mail," is a fascinating element in the love stories. Its power cannot be underestimated. Many couples corresponded for several years. Not only did the letters sustain relationships, they also enhanced and strengthened them. The cheerful, newsy letters from a Canadian bride or sweetheart did wonders for the morale of a lonely serviceman in a remote outpost. Many of these letters are treasured possessions to this day and are safely stored in family archives.

Although all the stories are different, there is a commonality among them. All of the war grooms have said that coming to Canada was one of the best decisions they ever made, and they became proud citizens. They praise their adopted country at every opportunity. Many have professed their love for their particular locales, which they say are the best places in the world to live. The war grooms in this book have had successful careers and have led productive lives. I continue to be amazed at the many skills and talents they brought to this country.

The war grooms were so grateful to the countless volunteers who made their wartime experiences in Canada enjoyable that many of them wanted "to give something back." Many became volunteers after they immigrated, and their services are legendary. In spite of the many horrendous events that occurred during World War II, some good things did result, and the war grooms are one of those good things.

Throughout this journey, I have received help from various sources. I particularly want to thank my husband, Verne, who has offered his advice and encouragement. My editor, Susan Code McDougall, has been most patient and helpful. Of course, I must acknowledge my deceased stepfather-in-law, Bill Thomas, who, unwittingly provided the inspiration for this book. I used to tease him, saying that one day I would write his story, and he would laugh. Little did he know! Several other people have helped me along the way, and I hesitate to name them all for fear that I may inadvertently omit some of them, but they know who they are. To all those wonderful people, "Thank you, thank you, thank you!"

All profits from the publication of this book (after all expenses, including publishing and marketing costs) will be donated to the following nonprofit organizations:

The Canadian War Museum in Ottawa
The Commonwealth Air Training Plan Museum in Brandon, Manitoba
The Western Canada Aviation Museum, Inc. in Winnipeg

Judy Kozar

THE BRITISH COMMONWEALTH AIR TRAINING PLAN

The BCATP was a massive air-training plan that involved Britain and many Commonwealth countries. Its impact on the war effort was huge. Because of the foresight of astute politicians and military strategists who were well aware of the threat from Nazi Germany, negotiations and planning for the BCATP began even before the war started. After preliminary negotiations, an agreement was signed in Ottawa by representatives from Great Britain, Canada, Australia, and New Zealand in December 1939.[3]

The British Air Ministry set up The Plan, and sent thousands of RAF personnel to Canada to open and operate the training schools. Their numbers were augmented by many civilians who helped to run the training schools. Great Britain was on the frontline of the air war and was not an ideal location for aircrew training. Canada had adequate fuel supplies, wide-open spaces, safe skies, and the industrial capacity to supply the training schools' requirements. It was agreed that airmen would receive preliminary training in their own countries before they were sent to Canada for advanced training. The number of aircrew graduates from the BCATP was 131,553.[4] The Plan was an astonishing feat of logistics.

A line of Tiger Moth training aircraft at Swift Current RAF base.
(Photo: Commonwealth Air Training Plan Museum)

---

[3] F.J. Hatch, *Aerodrome of Democracy: Canada and the British Commonwealth Air Training Plan 1939-1945* (Ottawa: Canadian Government Print Centre, 1983), p. 1.

[4] Dunmore, *Wings for Victory*, p. 361.

CARBERRY, MANITOBA, AND NO. 33 SFTS

Sixteen of the war grooms in this book either trained at No. 33 SFTS in Carberry or were part of the operational staff. That was just how it worked out. I didn't mean to favour any one province or one training school. I followed up on every lead I received.

The story of Carberry and its flying school is representational of the many training schools that operated throughout the country during World War II. There were twenty-nine service training flying schools, of which No. 33 SFTS was one. The BCATP also operated many other types of training schools, too: elementary flying training schools, air observer schools, air navigation schools, general reconnaissance schools, bombing and gunnery schools, wireless schools, operational training units, flying instructors schools, initial training schools, and several other specialist schools. I was told by some of the war grooms who were at No. 33 SFTS that the operational staff reached 1500 at its height. When one considers just how many schools were in operation, one can only imagine the number of individuals that were required to run them.

The station sign for No. 33 SFTS at Carberry, Manitoba.
(Photo: Commonwealth Air Training Plan Museum)

Many small communities throughout the country, still reeling from the economic effects of the Great Depression, wanted to be selected as sites for training schools. It was no secret that there were many economic benefits to be had when a training school was located in a community. Local businesses supplied building materials and other commodities. Many civilian jobs were created at the training school and in the community. The airmen patronized local businesses, such as restaurants, movie theatres, bowling alleys, stores, and beer parlours. Needless to say, the young ladies also welcomed the hundreds of eligible, attractive airmen to their communities. It was an interesting time.

The station crest for No. 33 SFTS at Carberry, Manitoba
(Photo: Commonwealth Air Training Plan Museum)

Carberry is a town in western Manitoba, approximately forty-eight kilometres east of Brandon, and 160 kilometres west of Winnipeg. Agriculture was and is the primary industry in the area. No. 33 SFTS at Carberry became operational on December 26, 1940, when the first draft of RAF staff members arrived. The school closed on November 17, 1944, after four years of operation. Even after its closure, the flying school at Carberry continued to stimulate the economy, at least indirectly. The site had a succession of owners who provided jobs for the local people. Currently, a potato-processing plant occupies the site and is the major employer in the area. A few of the original buildings from No. 33 still exist, and some of the runways can still be used for emergency landings. The people of Carberry have not forgotten No. 33 SFTS. It is part of the town's legacy.

A few of the locals bought some of the training planes after the school closed. Some were safely stored in barns, and many of those machines have been lovingly restored and are now in aviation museums. I have it on authority that some of the Ansons, however, became chicken coops and playhouses for children.

Much of the archival history of No. 33 has been safely stored in Carberry

Plains Archives. The Commonwealth Air Training Plan Museum in Brandon also has a wealth of information and memorabilia about No. 33, as well as other training stations.

The citizens of Carberry enjoyed having the airmen in their community, and the feeling was mutual. The men who trained in Carberry and who operated the school have never forgotten the hospitality of the warm, generous people who welcomed them into their community and into their homes. Many an old-timer still gets a warm, fuzzy feeling when talking about the training school and the boys in blue. This story was repeated in every community that had a BCATP training school. Thousands of airmen can attest to that!

Lana Turner sent a signed photograph of herself to the airmen at No. 33 SFTS.
(Photo: Commonwealth Air Training Plan Museum)

NORMAN (NORM) BEST

NELSON, BRITISH COLUMBIA

My husband, Norman Best, was born in Leeds, Yorkshire. He joined the RAF in 1939 when he was not quite eighteen and was one of the many airmen sent to Canada to maintain the planes that were used to train pilots. Norm was stationed in Medicine Hat, Alberta, at No. 34 Service Training Flying School and was an airframe mechanic.

The ladies in Nelson, British Columbia, wanted to help with the war effort. Since No. 34 was the closest training school, they invited the airmen to spend their leaves in their community. Whenever the airmen came to Nelson on leave, the ladies would make arrangements for them to stay with local families. The citizens welcomed the airmen with open arms and always tried to provide entertainment for them.

Norm was on leave in Nelson when I met him on a blind date that I did not want to go on. In June 1941, my friend Ruby met an RAF fellow in the park after a recruitment parade. They made plans to go canoeing that night and invited me to go along. Three on a date wasn't my idea of having fun, and I declined. I was no gooseberry! The RAF fellow insisted that I come along because he said he had a friend who would be just perfect for me. I pointed out that four in a canoe was not a good idea—anything to get out of going. I gave in and reluctantly agreed, on the condition that my date and I go in a separate canoe.

Norman and Lois Best during their honeymoon.
(Photo: Best Family)

Norman and Lois Best on their wedding day. (Photo: Best Family)

Norm, my blind date, was in the beer parlour at the time, and the RAF fellow sent word in so that he could come out to join us. The three of us waited and waited, but my date didn't make an appearance. Apparently, someone had organized entertainment for the airmen inside the beer parlour, and Norm was in no hurry to leave. Now, I have a very short fuse, and I became quite impatient with the whole ridiculous situation. I did not like waiting to go on a date that I was not crazy about in the first place. Even though women were not allowed to enter beer parlours in those days, I stood in the doorway and called out Norm's name. I said that if he didn't come out that minute, I was leaving. Needless to say, he rushed out.

Much to my surprise, I enjoyed myself on that blind date. We spent the evening paddling on the lake, and when Norm pulled over to the shore and got out, I was a little anxious. It took me a while to realize that he had been drinking a lot of beer and had to leave the canoe in order to relieve himself. We had such a good time that we didn't get back to my home until 2:30 in the morning. Norm was coughing, and I asked him if he wanted something for it. I knew nothing about mixing drinks in those days, and I poured him three-quarters of a glass of straight rye from my father's bottle. Norm told me later that he had difficulty finding his way home that night.

We corresponded while Norm was in Medicine Hat, and we saw each other when we could. As time went by, our relationship deepened, and we became engaged. We were married in May 1943, and although we invited only forty guests to the reception, the church was packed. My cousin, Velma Blaney, played the piano at our reception, and we had a grand party with all the RAF lads there. Our honeymoon was spent in Nelson, and we had a wonderful time just being together. Those long leisurely walks along the railroad tracks are some of my precious memories. We had no shortage of invitations for dinner from the good people in Nelson.

We lived in Medicine Hat for five short months as a married couple, and I really enjoyed shopping and planning the meals. Norm was always mowing somebody's lawn or helping people with other jobs around town. He was like that all his life, and even in his later years after he had a heart attack, he was out there building a deck for an elderly lady.

Norm was posted to England in January 1944. It was not unexpected, but it was a very sad time for us. After Norm left, I returned to Nelson and lived with my family. Norm had a short furlough with his parents in England and was then posted to various air bases in southern England. Prior to D-Day, he was seconded by the Navy, and he was also an air gunner after the Invasion.

Any correspondence during this time was sporadic, and when a letter did arrive, it was usually so severely censored that it made no sense. At other times, I would receive several letters on the same day.

The Royal Air Force encouraged spouses to come to England, and Norm arranged for me to follow. My pregnancy delayed my departure, however. When our son, John, was nine weeks old, we received our call. The baby was born with a glandular problem, which required treatment, but the doctor assured me that he was well enough for the journey. We left Nelson on November 23, 1944, on the train to Montreal. After three days there, we went to New York and boarded our ship, the *Rangatiki*, a former New Zealand pleasure ship that carried 700 passengers. Our first sailing was unsuccessful because of engine trouble, and we returned to port. A week later, on December 9, 1944, we sailed out of New York again, and we felt secure with our escort of thirty-five corvettes.

Our son did not do well on the journey with the changes of milk and water, and he cried a lot, especially at night. It was the rule that we had to sleep with our clothes on for safety reasons, but it was so warm on the ship, we were lucky to have our underwear on when the ship's steward called us to breakfast. The food on that ship was superb.

After ten days at sea, we finally arrived, but did not make the tide in time, so we spent one more night and day aboard the ship gazing wistfully at the dock in Liverpool. I still remember the frustrating wait. So near, and yet so far! It was a beautiful sight, however, to see the thirty-five corvettes sail away in one long line. In the meantime, Norm was very worried about us and couldn't understand why the trip was taking so long.

After docking in Liverpool, a New Zealand army officer was in charge of getting me through customs with my trunks and onto a train for Doncaster. I was shocked at the sight of Liverpool. It was a mess with fallen bricks everywhere. I missed my train connections and did not arrive at Doncaster until twelve hours later. Norm's family met the baby and me at the station. Norm had often talked about his family, and it was a lovely, warm experience to finally meet them.

Early the next morning, Norm got leave and rushed to his parents' home to greet us. What a wonderful feeling it was to be so lovingly held in his arms once again. It had been eleven months since he had left Canada on that cold January morning. Norm came to Doncaster as often as possible. It was always a surprise to see him, and the visits kept my spirits up.

My life in wartime Britain began in earnest. That winter, we could hear the bombing in Sheffield, and the next day's paper verified the attacks. On other nights, the windows in the house would shake as our planes flew overhead on their way to bomb Germany. It was a very dismal, cold winter, and the factories in the area gave off a lot of pollution. Blackouts are not something I would ever want to go through again, and the rationing was severe. We cherished any diversion that took our minds off our circumstances and never missed an opportunity to go to the movies, or flicks, as they were called then.

Everyone was so relieved when the war finally ended. Sadly, Norm left for occupational duty in Germany in May 1945, and we were separated once again. After several months, he was sent home and was discharged in September 1946. We resumed our lives, but we continued to live with Norm's parents because there were no homes available at that time. My mother sent out parcels regularly, and I shared this bounty with my appreciative in-laws. Even though the war was over, rationing continued, and there were shortages of just about everything.

We finally decided we had to start living on our own. We arranged to view a brand new bungalow at night by flashlight in an outlying village and purchased it. We started a part of our lives that turned out to be a total disaster. Everything seemed to go wrong for us that winter. The bus distance from Doncaster where we worked was long, I was laid off from my job, and Norm took ill with quinsy and flu and nearly died. It was one of England's coldest winters [1946–47]. Our new home leaked under the tiled roof, and the leakage caused the paint on the bedroom wall to run. It was so cold that the toilet would not flush unless there was a candle under the reservoir. Bath water was limited, and we had little coal for heat. Because Norm was so ill, I was the one who had to go into the attic where I balanced on the studs and scooped up buckets of snow that the neighbour's daughter would carry out for me. The doctor came every day to see Norm and gave him the new sulfa drug. On the final night of his illness, the doctor told me that the next few hours would determine whether or not he would live. Towards morning, Norm showed signs of recovery, and I was so relieved.

Eventually, the builder released us from our obligation because of the problems with the house. We then rented a room and shared facilities with another family. The flush toilet was outside, but we did have chamber pots. We eventually returned to Norm's family.

My parents made repeated requests for us to come to Canada, and in 1950, after long consideration, we were off on a new challenge and a better life. In Canada, Norm became a General Motors salesman and won several sales awards. In time, he had access to a Shell franchise, a part of his life he enjoyed immensely. Norm never regretted coming to Canada, and he always said it was one of the best decisions he ever made. We visited England in 1977, the only time that Norm ever returned.

In 1985, we moved to Sidney on Vancouver Island where Norm passed away in his sleep during our second year there. After Norm's death, I returned to Nelson where I have lived ever since. I have been back to England four times since and may try to visit one more time because I have two lovely nieces and their extended families there.

There are so many good times to remember, and Norm is still with me. I can't seem to leave him out of any activity. He is always in my thoughts.

Lois Best, June 2005

ART BOLTON

WINNIPEG, MANITOBA

I was born in Newton-le-Willows, Lancashire, which is now Merseyside since county re-alignment and volunteered for the RAF when I was eighteen. After some training in England, I came to Canada aboard the *Queen Elizabeth* to train as a navigator. Our ship docked in New York, and we were soon on the train to Moncton, New Brunswick, where we stayed for about a month before shipping out to No. 5 Air Observer School in Winnipeg. We were Course No. 82B, and between ground school, flying in Avro Ansons and taking potshots from behind our billet, we had a very enjoyable time before graduating on December 24, 1943.

I met my future wife during this training spell on a blind date. One of my friends was dating a Winnipeg girl, who had a friend named Daphne Gagg. On our first date, we all went to a well-known nightclub called The Cave.

We dated seriously for about two months before the time came for me to be posted to England. I had Christmas at Daphne's home before leaving for Moncton on Boxing Day. However, there was no ship available and rather than stay in Moncton, I was able to return to Winnipeg and to Daphne for two weeks. By this time, I realized that Daphne was very special to me. I was sent back again to Moncton, but, again, with no hope of a ship. Again, I returned to Winnipeg and to Daphne for another two weeks. After this visit, a ship was finally available in Moncton, and we sailed off to England. I didn't return to Canada until 1946. During the intervening years, hundreds of letters passed between us.

In England, after several courses at various bases, we were posed to Mildenhall, which had been an RAF station for many years. Accommodations were great there, especially after I was commissioned and moved to the officers' mess. Prior to that, in the NCO billets, we were limited to a very small supply of coal for the fireplace in winter. That situation called for midnight raids on the local coal yard to supplement our meagre supply. Most fortunately, we were never spotted on these excursions, or my commission would have been in jeopardy.

Meanwhile, the war continued, and I was posted to active duty with Bomber Command. At Upper Heyford, I met the rest of my crew, and we were a rather mixed bunch. Our pilot was from Oakland, California, our wireless operator was from Brisbane, Australia, and the rest of us were from England. Our bomb aimer was from Watford, and the two gunners were from Yorkshire and Scotland. Our pilot had joined the RAF before the U.S.A. became involved in the war and could have transferred to the U.S. Air Force, but he chose to stay with us. We finished thirty trips over Germany, and we were lucky to suffer only a few shrapnel holes and a slight injury to our upper gunner. We never definitely observed a German fighter, although our rear gunner called for evasive action on a couple of occasions when he thought that he spotted a fighter on our tail.

After our tour of operations, we were all split up, and I was posted to Transport Command in India and Burma. This posting required additional navigational training, and I spent time at Castle Donnington where a New Zealand pilot, two other English airmen, and I made up the crew. We eventually flew out to Poona, India. We spent a couple of days in Cairo with engine trouble, and we were able to visit the pyramids and the Sphinx.

While in Poona, we were with No. 10 Squadron, flying all over India, but the majority of flights were between Madras and Bombay. We ferried our troops to the ships that took them back to the U.K. Another interesting time was when we were detailed to fly the Australian Test Cricket Team around India for games. I also remember one Christmas when a group of us commandeered the station steamroller and drove that around the station. Fortunately, there was no serious damage, although most of us were a little under the influence. Because the squadron CO was a participant, we avoided any charges.

When the Eastern War ended, we were moved for a while to Burma where our job was primarily to drop rice supplies to the local people because the Japanese had burned their crops. While there, I had occasion to fly with another crew one day when their regular navigator was ill. The next day, he was back on the job, but his plane and two others did not return from their trip. It took almost a week to find them. All were killed except for one Ghurka who was along to heave rice bags from the plane. Apparently, all three planes had flown into a closed valley and had no room to turn around. They all crashed into the mountain side. That loss was greater than any loss we incurred over Germany with No. 15 Squadron.

We were back to Poona for a while before being posted to Rawalpindi in northern India where our job was to fly a regiment of Ghurkas over to an area for parachute drop training. We were all offered the opportunity to do a parachute drop ourselves, but only our pilot took them up on it.

My demobilization number eventually came up, and I was flown to Karachi where

I received my orders to command a troop train returning a load of our troops to Bombay. This train took the long way around to avoid the worst of the heat in the desert, but even so, conditions in the carriages were very poor, and at one stop, there was almost a rebellion by the troops. It was averted only when the servicemen were reminded that any trouble would only delay their return home.

After a few days in Bombay, I was aboard the *Samaria*, where I was the commanding officer of a troop deck for the almost four-week journey home. After arriving in Liverpool, we were off to the demobilization station and were home a day later. I was soon in touch with a friend from my earlier days in the RAF who had connections at Cunard, and through him, I was able to get passage on the *Franconia*. I was finally back in Winnipeg by December 1946.

Before leaving the RAF, it was suggested that I take an accounting position after returning to civilian life. However, my first job in Winnipeg was with the CNR at their Osborne Street shops as a trainee mechanic. Because they would not recognize my three years of training in this type of work before the war, my stay there was only about six months. I left for a job that got me into book-keeping, and ultimately, accounting. I stayed in this line of work until I retired as a business manager at a medical clinic in 1986.

Daphne and I were married at St. John's Cathedral on November 5, 1949, Guy Fawkes Day. The British always remember that date because it is a celebration of the

Thumbing a ride. Airmen from No. 33 SFTS on leave.
(Photo: Commonwealth Air Training Plan Museum)

Gunpowder Plot to blow up Parliament. I was well received by Daphne's parents, and although my parents were not happy to see me go to Canada, they realized that I was leaving for a better life than England could offer at the time. Daphne and I have been back to England on eight occasions. I have been a Canadian citizen since 1950.

I have no regrets about choosing Canada as my home. My transition was helped by membership in the Winnipeg RAF Club, which was comprised of many ex-RAF lads in the same boat as I. Unfortunately, there are not too many of those members left now. I subsequently joined the Winnipeg Wartime Pilots' and Observers' Association, which was comprised of aircrew members who trained with the British Commonwealth Air Training Plan. The majority of members are in Canada, but others are located in the U.S.A., Great Britain, Australia, New Zealand, Mexico, and the West Indies. This group is also decreasing because of the grim reaper.

I lost touch with both my crews after the war, but eventually, suffering a little nostalgia, I located several of them. My pilot from No.15 Squadron stayed in the RCAF as a physical education instructor, and I met him once in Winnipeg with his wife. He passed away a few years later. I visited my rear gunner a couple of times in England, but the last time that I saw him, he was in a nursing home, and he died the day after I saw him. My wireless operator came over from Australia for one of the reunions that the Wartime Pilots sponsored, and we spent a week together. Unfortunately, he passed away a couple of years ago. I located my New Zealand pilot in Dunedin, and a friend visited him, but I have not been to that area at all. He has since passed away. I have been unable to locate any others, and doubt if any are still around.

June 2005

ROD BOURKE

CHILLIWACK, BRITISH COLUMBIA

I was born in Pahiatua (Maori name for "home of the gods"), New Zealand, in 1921. My three brothers, my sister, and I were brought up on a sheep farm.

When war broke out in 1939, I applied to the RNZAF to train as a pilot, but was rejected because I was, supposedly, colour-blind. A few months later, I was conscripted into the army and passed the same vision test that I failed in the air force. Thanks to a neighbour who was in the Air Force Reserve, I was able to have a retest and started training as a pilot in 1941.

Our initial training was carried out at New Plymouth Airport in New Zealand on Tiger Moths. After going solo and putting in fifty hours of flying, I qualified to go to Canada to do my service flying training. We were transported on a beautiful American cruise ship, the *Mariposa*, to San Francisco in early October, but we made several stops on the way, some of which were Fiji, Tahiti, Pago Pago, and Honolulu. The Golden Gate Bridge in San Francisco magically appeared out of the fog as our ship approached the harbour. The entire voyage was a fantastic experience.

We took the train from San Francisco to Vancouver, where we had a short stopover. I was sitting on the old post office steps in Vancouver looking a bit homesick when Mrs. MacDonald, a dear Scottish lady, approached. She asked my name and where I was going. We were not supposed to divulge that information, but I did, and a little later, a box of delicious shortbread arrived for me along with a letter.

We boarded the train again, this time bound for Saskatoon. The wooden seats on the train were hard, but the meals and service were fantastic. It was a rude awakening for us, however, when we arrived in Saskatoon on a cold, November morning. Although we were without proper winter clothing, we were put into the back of an open truck and driven to the station. The prairie winter was an eye-opener for us, since there was no snow to speak of in New Zealand.

We started our course on Cessna Cranes on November 10, 1941. Just five days later, I made my first solo flight, and until December 30, it was regular flying. This all came to a screeching halt when I was rushed to hospital with acute appendicitis on New Year's Eve. After my operation and two weeks in hospital, I had one month's sick leave. I contacted Mrs. MacDonald in Vancouver, the lady who gave me the shortbread, and she kindly agreed to put me up during my leave. It was a wonderful experience, and I was really spoiled by her and Meg, her daughter. It was wonderful to see green grass, rain, mountains and the overall beauty of Vancouver after a couple of months of freezing, snowy weather in Saskatoon.

I returned to Saskatoon in mid-February and started flying again. All went well, and I was awarded my wings about April 20. I remember one exciting event that took place on April 13. One of the instructors took three of us on a cross-country trip to Medicine Hat, Alberta. I ran out of gas twenty miles short of base and landed in a plowed field with the plane undamaged. I understand the instructor was disciplined.

Several other New Zealand pilots and I were sent to Halifax, Nova Scotia. We naturally expected to be sent to the U.K. Instead, after sitting around in Halifax for three weeks, we were advised that there were too many pilots and a shortage of planes in England, so we were to spend a short time waiting in Canada. We were posted to No. 122 Composite Squadron at Patricia Bay on Vancouver Island. We were, of course, very disappointed when we didn't get overseas, but I was thrilled with Pat Bay because it was close to beautiful Vancouver.

Rod and Marj Bourke on their wedding day.
(Photo: Bourke Family)

We flew Lysanders, Norsemen and, occasionally, Bolingbrokes while at Pat Bay until March 1943. It was a great experience, and it was during this period that I got to meet my future wife at a wonderful resort called Yellowpoint Lodge on Vancouver Island.

Marjorie Smith, who was working at the Bank of Montreal, and some friends had come over from Vancouver for a holiday, and three of us Kiwis had gone to the Lodge for a few days. We all met at the Lodge, and Marj and I hit it off right from the start. Over the next few months, we tried to spend as much time together as possible. Marj introduced me to her family, and I had many wonderful meals cooked by Mrs. Smith. I really put my foot in my mouth when I informed Mrs. Smith at Thanksgiving that the turkey was "the finest piece of pork I had ever tasted." I had never eaten turkey before, and it was unfamiliar to New Zealanders. Marj and I spent a wonderful New Year's Eve together with another couple at Yellowpoint Lodge. All good things came to an end, however, and I was posted overseas in March 1943.

I didn't hold out much hope of seeing Marj again, but we kept in touch periodically during the time I took my operational training course and while I was flying Mosquitoes with No. 488 (NZ) Night Fighter Squadron. We were stationed mainly in the south of England until after the Invasion, and then we were posted to Amiens in France in September 1944. Later, the squadron moved to Holland where we were stationed until the end of April 1945 when the squadron was disbanded. We were back in London in time to celebrate VE Day, an experience never to be forgotten!

As the war was winding down, a circular came out from RNZAF Headquarters. Apparently, those of us who had trained in Canada could return there if we got letters from Canadian girls indicating that they would marry us. I wrote a letter and asked Marj to marry me, and much to my surprise and delight, she promptly said, "Yes." I travelled to Halifax by ship and took the train right across Canada to Vancouver. Marjorie, in a lovely pink coat, her family, Mrs. MacDonald, and Meg were there to meet me at the old CN station. What a thrill it was! Marj and I were married, and we spent our honeymoon at the Vancouver Hotel, the Empress Hotel in Victoria, and finally, at Yellowpoint Lodge where we had first met back in 1942.

It was several months before transportation to New Zealand could be arranged for the grooms from New Zealand. Our wives would follow us to New Zealand at a later date. Eventually, a freighter took me and other grooms to Tahiti where we stayed for a few days. We finally disembarked in New Caledonia. Because we were still a long way from New Zealand, the air force sent flying boats to transport us the rest of the way. The journey took six very long weeks. My entire family, including my brother, Denny, who had returned from service in the Pacific Islands, was on hand to greet me at the station. The celebration lasted for many days.

Our Canadian brides left Vancouver six weeks after we did and sailed directly to Auckland on another freighter. Poor Marj was pregnant at the time and was seasick the entire way. It was wonderful to see her after three months. We spent a couple of days in Auckland, and then we took the train down to my home for another great reunion. My family loved Marj, and she adapted very quickly to farm life. My mother took delight in taking Marj to town every Tuesday to meet her friends.

I was discharged from the RNZAF in February 1946, and we stayed with my family until our son was born. Unfortunately, the poor lad was born with spina bifida and was transferred to the hospital in Wellington. Marj and I moved there to be with him. We were fortunate to stay with a fellow airman from my Vancouver Island days. The baby passed away in late July, and it was a devastating blow to us all.

I was working at odd jobs around Wellington and started university, when I heard from Marj's father that I had a good chance to become a pilot for one of the lumber companies in British Columbia. We packed up and returned to Vancouver. It wasn't easy in 1947 to get transportation to North America from New Zealand. After several false starts, I was able to get Marj on a Pan American plane in April. After making three or four stops along the way, she arrived safely in Vancouver in time to give birth to our daughter, Maureen, at the end of June. In the meantime, I was able to land a job on a freighter that was taking farm animals as far as Tahiti.

Working on a ship that transported farm animals was an interesting experience. Cows started to calve and had to be milked. The beautiful Hereford cattle wouldn't eat or drink, and the pigpen smell was absolutely unbearable. However, it was clear sailing after Tahiti, and Vancouver was a welcome sight in mid-October. I hadn't seen Marj for six months, and our daughter was more than three months old when I first saw her.

The flying job didn't work out, since the company that serviced the plane had just laid off their pilots for the winter. Instead of flying for a living up and down the B.C. coast, I ended up working in the quality control department of that company. I took courses in lumber grading and realized it was a field I was quite happy to be in, and that there was a future in it. In time, I became an inspector with the Pacific Lumber Inspection Bureau. After staying in Vancouver for four years, we moved to Vancouver Island.

In 1960, I was offered a job with Cariboo Lumber Manufacturers' Association in Williams Lake. It was a good opportunity that included a substantial increase in salary and the use of a company car. Williams Lake was a small village in those days, but the people were wonderful. It didn't take long before Marj had made many friends. She became active in the hospital auxiliary and had no trouble keeping busy.

Our daughter, Maureen, became a teacher. She and her husband John moved to Chilliwack where John went into the jewelry business with his father, and Maureen taught school. They had two children. In 1986, we decided to move to Chilliwack to be close to our family.

Marj and I made our first visit to New Zealand in 1963 and made several more trips over the years. In the 1970s, many of our relatives started to come to Canada to visit us. In 1990, Marj was not well because of heart problems, but was determined to go through with the New Zealand trip. We got the doctor's permission, and we were both glad that we made the trip, Marj's last.

On December 1, 1990, we had just finished our pizza about 6:00 p.m. Marj had gone into the living room, and I took a cup of tea in to her. I went back for cookies, and when I returned, she was slumped over. The ambulance people tried to bring her around, but to no avail. I had lost my dear Marj. Though it was a terrific shock at the time, I realize now that it was a great way to go. She was a wonderful girl, and I was very fortunate to have had her as my loving wife. I will never forget the city girl who followed me to a New Zealand sheep farm. Ruth, my second wife, and I are in good health and enjoy living in beautiful British Columbia.

September 2006

JIM BRADY

WINNIPEG, MANITOBA

Jim was a Scot right from Glasgow. He joined the RAF during the war and was a member of the groundcrew sent to Canada as part of the British Commonwealth Air Training Plan. Before he left Britain, all the airmen on the ship had been issued desert clothing. We never knew if this was an accident or if the British government was trying to confuse German spies on the dock. Jim's job was to help to maintain and repair the planes that were used for training. He was posted to No. 33 SFTS in Carberry, Manitoba, and was there from 1940 to 1943.

Strange as it seems, we met at my parents' home in St. James [suburb of Winnipeg] in May 1941. Jim happened to be the best man at my sister's wedding. She also had a war groom husband, but they both have passed away. What attracted me to Jim was his thick Scottish accent, which I loved.

Jim and his friends would sometimes spend their leaves in Winnipeg. It seems unbelievable now, but a group of airmen would hire a taxi to bring them to Winnipeg, which is over 100 miles away. We went together for a while, but we didn't have much money to go to expensive places. Jim was part of the groundcrew and did not receive officer's pay. Neither of us were dancers, but we did go to the occasional movie. We both loved to go for walks, and, as a matter of fact, Jim proposed on one of those long walks.

We were married in my parents' home on September 26, 1942. After our wedding, we spent the night in a hotel, and then we left for Carberry by train the next morning. I remember the morning of our departure very well because we nearly froze when the temperature dropped suddenly. All our winter clothes had been shipped ahead to Carberry.

Jim found us an apartment in a house in Carberry on Main Street. All during that October, the weather was beautiful, and we were so happy just being together. I have such fond memories of our time in Carberry when we were newlyweds.

Our first winter together was extremely cold with lots of snow, and one thermometer registered minus fifty degrees one night. We were not sure if this was an accurate reading, but it certainly was a shock to see the thermometer. Jim was working nights during that time, and he walked home from the base to Carberry in that intense cold, a distance of two miles.

We went to Winnipeg for Christmas, and after we got back to Carberry, rumours were flying that Jim would be sent to a war zone. The rumours were correct, and he was transferred back to Britain in 1943. We corresponded until he returned in 1946, three years later. During this time, Jim was stationed at various bases in Britain, but I can no longer remember the names of them now. While he was gone, I worked in a drugstore, and I lived with my sister.

While Jim was in Carberry, he received Canadian wages. After he was posted to Britain, he received British wages, which were a lot less, but even so, he sent three-quarters of his pay to me. That came to the grand total of $48 a month. We never did have much money in those days, but it didn't seem to matter because we were so much in love.

The war finally ended, and Jim knew that his future was in Canada. He never even considered staying in Scotland. Except for one year in California, we lived our entire married lives in Winnipeg. Jim worked as a sales representative for Pritchard Engineering Company, and he retired when he was sixty-five. He became a Canadian citizen in the 1950s, but I can't remember the exact date. Jim loved Canada, and the cold climate never bothered him.

Jim's father had died before he emigrated to Canada, and his mother was very angry with him because he married a Canadian girl. I tried to reach out to her,

Dealing with a prairie winter at No. 33 SFTS required constant vigilance.
(Photo: Commonwealth Air Training Plan Museum)

*Airmen from No. 33 SFTS still
talk about the day the temperature
dipped to -50 degrees*
(Photo: Commonwealth Air Training Plan Museum)

but she never did answer any of my letters. After a while, I gave up. Jim never returned to Scotland after he came to Canada in 1946. We never seemed to be able to put money aside for a trip, and there didn't seem to be any reason to return, given the situation with his mother. Jim lost contact with the rest of the family for a long time, but fortunately, he did re-establish contact with one sister in later years. She still phones me to this day, and I look forward to our conversations.

I was born in St. James; I was married in St. James; and I still live in St. James. Needless to say, I have no desire to live anywhere else. Jim and I were married for sixty-one years until he died two years ago, and I miss him so much. My three children, six grandchildren, and two great-grandchildren bring me much happiness.

Wyn Brady, May 2005

Tom Brock

I'm from Ayrshire, Scotland, and I joined the RAF in 1939. I will always remember one incident that happened shortly after I enlisted. In 1940, I was the flight engineer on a Lockheed Hudson. We were over the North Sea approaching the coast of Scotland when I tried to get the wheels of the aircraft down in order to land. I discovered, to my horror, that there was no hydraulic pressure. I poured a pint of hydraulic fluid into the line, but that didn't help much. We had two flasks of tea and one flask of coffee. I poured those into the line, too, and the wheels came halfway down. I passed the empty flasks around to the crew and asked for donations of urine. I poured the crew's contributions into the line, and our co-operative effort worked. Fortunately, the wheels came all the way down, and we were able to land safely. The only down side to the episode, however, was that I had to spend three days cleaning out the system. The leak had been caused by a split rubber seal.

In 1941, I was scheduled for overseas duty. We knew we were probably going to the American side of the Atlantic because we had to give up our gas masks when we boarded the ship. After arriving in Halifax, we got on a westbound train. I opened the train window to get some fresh air and, to my surprise, it froze in that position all the way to Carberry, Manitoba. That was my first taste of a Canadian winter.

I was part of the operational staff at No. 33 SFTS in Carberry where I worked as an airframe fitter for the planes that were used to train pilots. Once, when I was on leave in Brandon, I was billeted with an Irish family whose son was in the RCAF. While I was there, I went to a dance at the Brandon Armouries, an event that was to change the entire course of my life. There, I would meet Agnes Burton who was called "Bubbles" by her friends and family. After I got to know her, I called her "Bubs."

At that time, Bubs was a seventeen-year old student in her final year at Brandon Collegiate and was in the midst of her June examinations. Wanting desperately to go to the Saturday dance at the Armouries, she promised her parents that she would study hard the following Sunday for her chemistry final on Monday morning. They agreed, and Bubs was allowed to attend the dance.

Bubs had a sister also at the dance, and she was dating an RAF fellow. Bubs had told her sister that she was going to marry me after she spotted me across the dance floor, but I didn't find this out until later in our courtship. Of course, everybody at the dance laughed when they heard Bubs make this comment. She asked her sister's date to introduce her to me, and I was very glad that that he did. After the dance, I walked Bubs home, and we made arrangements to meet again.

Tom and Agnes (Bubbles) Brock on their wedding day.
(Photo: Brock Family)

The following day, Bubs surprised her family when she said that she had met the man she was going to marry. Well, as it happened, she failed the chemistry exam. Upon hearing the results of the exam, her dad said that there must have been a different chemistry happening at the dance. When I told my billeting family that I met Bubs at the dance, I was informed that she was a good girl, and they gave their approval.

Ironically, years later, I learned that Bubs had never liked the name Tom, nor was she fond of the Scottish accent. Then I came along and changed her perception.

Bubs and I became engaged that Christmas and were married on April 25, 1942. Jean, a friend of Bubs, was also engaged to an RAF fellow named John Hall. Bubs' parents gave both couples a double wedding, although there wasn't much money for anything too extravagant. Fortunately, friends, neighbours, and relatives pitched in, and the four of us were married in the family home in Brandon.[5] Although Bubs was Anglican, the Anglican minister wouldn't come to the home to marry us. Fortunately, the local Baptist minister was more accommodating and performed the wedding ceremonies. I returned to the U.K. in December 1943. At first, I was with a transport squadron near Manchester and, later, I was posted to various stations in Scotland. Our job was to transport food and supplies to the

---

[5] See John Hall's story.

outer islands of Scotland. Our crew happened to be flying off the coast of Holland when we received word of the D-Day invasion. My Dutch pilot was so excited about the news that he wanted to land in Holland, and he had to be reminded that it was still occupied by the Germans.

Because we didn't want to be separated for too long, Bubs came to the U.K. in July 1944 on a New Zealand troop ship. The passengers slept in hammocks, and Bubs couldn't turn over because the girl in the hammock directly above her was fairly hefty and weighed the hammock down to within a few inches of her nose.

Bubs arrived at Liverpool and took the train to Carlisle. There, she had to find her luggage and board another train to Glasgow. In all the confusion, she lost her gas mask. My adjutant informed me of my wife's arrival half an hour before she was due, and I rushed to meet her. Before she came to the U.K., Bubs had to agree to do war work and was assigned to a hospital in Scotland mending hospital gowns and sheets. Everything had to be recycled during wartime. She got her first electric kettle and her first pressure cooker in Scotland, although her washing machine was the scrub board. Our son was born on September 26, 1946.

I was discharged from the RAF in 1947, and I wanted to return to Canada as soon as possible. Surprisingly, my family took this announcement very well, but we had a problem arranging transportation. In the meantime, I worked for a Scottish aviation company. Because of my job, I learned that a converted Lancaster was scheduled to fly to Canada empty, and, fortunately, I was able to obtain permission for the three of us to fly in it. Bubs had only three hours' notice of the flight, but

The RAF hockey team. Sporting activities were an integral part of life at No. 33 SFTS.
(Photo: Carberry Plains Archives)

she rose to the occasion. At the time, lamb chops were cooking, and the baby's wash was drying on the line. The druggist solved our diaper problem. He provided us with special packing material that could be put inside some muslin diapers. These primitive disposable diapers did the trick.

I had always enjoyed the Service and wanted to continue in this line of work. I joined the RCAF after I came to Canada and retired in 1969. At the beginning of my service career with the RCAF, I was classified as Aircraftsman 2nd Class, and by the time I retired, I was a captain (Armed Forces Re-organization Act). Throughout my time in the Canadian Forces, I served in various capacities at several places: Air Force Headquarters, Ottawa (on Appointment to Commission), Central Officer School in Centralia (Training), and Air Force Headquarters (Staff Officer-Personnel). When I was at Rockcliffe, I was Staff Officer Quality Control, Methods, Analysis and Training; Staff Security officer; Staff Officer—Aero Section; and Technical Advisor to RCAF Materiel Laboratory Training School. My final posting before retirement was at Canadian Forces Headquarters in Ottawa, where we have lived ever since.

After my Air Force days were over, I worked for the government for sixteen years, after which I retired for good. I have no regrets about coming to Canada, and we have had a good life here. Bubs and I have been married for sixty-three years, and we are still very much in love. We have a son and a daughter, five grandchildren and four great-grandchildren.

October 2005

JAMES (JIM) COLVINE

WINNIPEG, MANITOBA

My late husband, Jim Colvine, was born in Darnchester, Scotland, on December 6, 1919. He joined the RAF shortly after the war started. He was posted overseas and ended up in Carberry, Manitoba, at No. 33 SFTS where he serviced the engines for the training aircraft.

Jim was on leave in Winnipeg when he and I met. Community dances were held almost every night at the Normandy Hall on Sherbrook Street, and I happened to be at one when I met this handsome, fun-loving airman with a wonderful Scottish brogue. He asked me to dance, and I was bowled over by his wonderful sense of humour. The fact that he was such a good dancer didn't hurt either. We seemed to click right away, and he asked me for a date. As I recall, we went to the Roseland Night Club on our first date, and from then on, we kept seeing each other whenever Jim was in Winnipeg. After we dated for a while, I brought Jim home, and my parents liked him right off. After that, Jim spent every one of his leaves at my home in Winnipeg, courting me. As time went by, he asked me to marry him, and, of course, I accepted. The wedding took place at Knox United Church in Winnipeg on October 9, 1943. After the wedding, Jim returned to Carberry, but it wasn't long before he was posted to the U.K. We said our tearful good-byes on January 3, 1944.

Jim and Marjorie Colvine on their wedding day.
(Photo: Colvine Family)

I was determined to go to Britain to be with Jim, but I had to wait until August 3, 1944, before I got the call. It took a while to get passage because most of the ships were being used to support the invasion in Normandy. A ship finally became available, but the voyage took three long weeks because we were diverted to the Azores to avoid German U-boats. After we docked in Liverpool, I proceeded to my in-laws' home, which at that time was at Sunilaw Station House, Northumberland, in northern England. Jim's family was absolutely wonderful to me, but I had difficulty understanding the Scottish accent at first. It was almost like listening to another language. My mother-in-law and I got along famously. In fact, when Jim and I returned to Canada later on, my mother-in-law said that she missed me more than she did Jim.

During the war, Jim was based at several locations in England, and I followed him around from place to place. I thoroughly enjoyed my time in Britain, in spite of the rationing, the blackouts, and the air-raid sirens. I was young, and I thought that the whole experience was one big holiday. The people I met were wonderful, the countryside in rural England was beautiful, and I was in love. Who could ask for more?

One incident stands out in my memory during my time in Britain. My brother was in the Canadian army and had been wounded during the fighting in Belgium. He was evacuated to England and was hospitalized there. I got word about his condition, and I proceeded to the Canadian hospital to visit him. As it turned out, he was recovering nicely from his wounds, and I was so relieved. We had a good visit, and it was great to hear a Canadian accent again. Because the hospital was on a Canadian army base, I was treated to a Coke, an unheard of treat in wartime Britain. I can still remember the experience after all these years. I have never tasted anything before or since that was so good!

Eventually, the war ended, but Jim wasn't demobilized until June 12, 1946. There was no doubt in Jim's mind where he wanted to spend the rest of his life. Canada was where he wanted to be, and that's where we went as soon as we could, via the old *Aquitania*. The voyage was very rough, and that is an understatement! I was seasick and flat on my back the whole way. I was rather surprised because my first crossing to Britain had been quite calm. We arrived in Halifax on New Year's Eve, and it wasn't soon enough for me! It was so wonderful to be able to have a solid surface under my feet again. We took the train to Winnipeg where we received a warm welcome from my family. Jim found employment at a machinery company after we arrived in Winnipeg, and eventually we bought a house and started a family.

Jim raved about Canada to his family back in Scotland, and after hearing about the wonders of his adopted country, they decided to emigrate, too. Jim's sister came to Canada first and settled in Kelowna, British Columbia, and his parents followed.

Later, his brother and his family, not wanting to be left behind, also joined their family in Canada. None of them ever regretted their decisions to move here.

Jim's parents arrived in the midst of a cold, prairie winter, and were staying with us until they went on to Kelowna to be with their daughter. On her first night in Canada, my mother-in-law put her hair net on the windowsill, as she always did back in Scotland. In the morning, she discovered that her precious hairnet had frozen solid to the windowsill. She couldn't believe it. Welcome to Manitoba!

My father-in-law was also in for a shock. Anyone who has experienced a prairie winter knows that there is a cloud of ice fog by the doorway when it is opened during extreme temperatures. It is similar to the exhaust from cars during the winter. Shortly after my father-in-law arrived at our home, he disappeared after the door was opened, and we couldn't find him. Apparently, he had seen the ice fog at the doorway and had gone into the basement to look for the source of the fire! It was many years before he lived that one down. In spite of the winters, Jim's family loved Canada as much as he did. My father-in-law always said that he should have come to Canada fifty years sooner.

Our son, Allan, was born in 1947, and our daughter, Lori, was born in 1956. Sadly, my husband succumbed to a fatal heart attack in 1972 after a wonderful life in Canada. There are several grandchildren and great-grandchildren now, but Jim was only able to enjoy his granddaughter, who was one-and-a-half years old, when he died.

Marjorie Colvine, December 2006

Douglas (Doug) Daws

KAMLOOPS, BRITISH COLUMBIA

In February 1941, I was notified by the RAF that I was to leave England because of an overseas posting. On the MS *Batory*, I was seasick for the first and only time in my life, and I mean really seasick! When I was standing beside the rail, wishing I would die, I passed out. Strangely, I was not seasick ever again in my life. On board, we were told that we were to open and staff a flying training school, which turned out to be No. 34 SFTS, located outside of Medicine Hat, Alberta.

After arriving in Halifax, we boarded a train that stopped in Montreal for a while. While we were there, our commanding officer said that we should get some exercise. He reassured us that he knew his way around because he had visited Montreal before. We all fell in and marched off. Eventually, our CO called a halt at an intersection where there was a policeman, and it was obvious from the gestures that he was being given directions. With the help of the policeman, we found our way back to the train station.

On our journey west, we were impressed by the vastness of the country and the amount of snow. We had a chance to leave the train for an hour or so near Thunder Bay, but no one could stay outside at that temperature for more than two minutes.

With all the news of the Battle of Britain, we were looked upon as heroes by the people of Medicine Hat, and many of us were adopted by the local families. The Askew family adopted Phil Stevens and me. Phil was a pretty good piano player, and we spent many happy evenings with Phil on the piano, me singing, and the family providing food.

The wonderful people in Medicine Hat were always looking out for us. They arranged for us to borrow ice skates. Few of us could skate, however, and the arena was a source of entertainment for the onlookers who laughed at the boys in blue trying to stand up. The citizens also set up The Empire Club. We could go there each afternoon and evening to read, write, and listen to music.

While in Medicine Hat, we had fallen into a pattern that was very pleasant. We rode bikes and played soccer on the field near the base. There was a movie house in town, as well as a couple of beer parlours. Musical programs, concerts and plays were also held at the base. A dance band was formed, and I was called upon to do the vocals. There was no shortage of entertainment, believe me. There was always something to do.

The serious business of No. 34 was, of course, flight training. When the weather was good, flight training took place twenty-four hours a day. During the harsh winters, aircraft had to be pushed into hangars to warm up before the engines would turn over. Normally, forty student pilots would be in each course, and the goal was to graduate one course each month. During the life of No. 34, which closed in November of 1944, forty-nine airmen lost their lives because of flying accidents.

My mother had a sister in Watrous, Saskatchewan, and I received an invitation in July 1941 to visit and to bring a friend. There is absolutely no doubt that this was the turning point of my life. Waiting for me at the bus stop were my Aunt Florence and a beautiful woman in a blue dress wearing a wide-brimmed blue hat, a picture that will be engraved in my memory until the end of my life. It was my cousin, Margaret Helen, or Madge for short. We were treated royally, and I tried to spend as much time as I could with Madge. I returned to Medicine Hat, but I often thought about the beautiful girl back in Watrous.

I had been corresponding with Madge since leaving Watrous, and to my great delight, I received a letter saying that she was coming to Medicine Hat to work at Eaton's. I purchased a record player for her suite and began a collection of records of the popular music of that time. Madge hosted friends of mine from No. 34, and we spent many wonderful evenings there.

In the spring of 1943, I was advised that I was one of the group to be repatriated to England. I did broach the subject of marriage a number of times, but Madge put me off, saying, "You go back to England, and we will see after the war." After a tearful farewell, I suffered through the long journey to Moncton. There, I learned that there was to be a long delay because of U-boat activity, and I decided to take the bull by the horns. I asked the unit chaplain for his support to return to Medicine Hat to marry Madge. The chaplain spoke to the CO who granted me a ten-day leave and a rail pass. I sent a telegram to Madge, telling her that I was returning to marry her, and that I had permission from the RAF. How relieved, pleased and gloriously happy I was to see Madge waiting for me with the news that the wedding arrangements had been made.

Madge had asked her friend, Ella Steele, and Bill Simpson, a friend of mine from No. 34, to attend the ceremony. The four of us walked to St. Barnabas Anglican Church on August 18, 1943, for the service which took place with borrowed rings, which did not detract one bit from our happiness. I was so fortunate to have this beautiful bride declare that she would be mine until death. For the celebration, we went to a small café for a simple meal, and we returned to Madge's flat for coffee and cake. A two-day honeymoon at Madge's suite was heaven to me, but it was all over much too soon.

When I got to Halifax, I was surprised to learn that I was to sail on the *Queen Elizabeth*. We were all given a two-week leave after we got to England, and I went to Cambridge where my mother was living after she was bombed out in Coventry. Everything was lost in the house in Coventry, including all my pre-war belongings. Fortunately, the family had taken shelter under the stairs.

I was posted to a radar station at Dengey-in-the-Marsh. Soon, orders came to report to a special services unit near Henley-on-Thames. This station was a taxi service to and from France. Just about every night, Lysanders ferried underground operatives and equipment to and from occupied territory.

In December 1943, I was posted to RAF Station Hawkshill Down in Kent. It was a low-level radar unit located on top of the chalk cliffs. When the weather was clear, one could see Calais on the French coast, but, unfortunately, the Germans could see us, too. They made our lives interesting with their Big Bertha guns. There was one occasion when a shell had a direct hit on a radar site hut when WAAF [Women's Auxiliary Air Force] operators were on duty, and all were killed. Being in that particular hot spot, we were subjected to air raids by the Germans and interception activities by the RAF and the army. The RAF would attack approaching German aircraft over the Channel, and then the army would have a go with their ack-ack guns.

At this time, the Germans started sending flying buzz bombs [V1s]. We could hear them coming, and then the coastal guns would open up on them. The drill was to find cover and wait for an explosion. The next nasty weapon was the V2.

In the midst of all this excitement, I received a message from the RAF indicating that my wife would be arriving in the near future. The news meant that I had to obtain permission for Madge to enter the restricted area. In addition, I had to make arrangements for new accommodations. Several days later, Madge still hadn't come, so I went to the cinema located on the sea front. During the show, we were told that all service personnel were to report immediately to their units. When I left the cinema, seeing all kinds of ships and floating devices in the Channel as far as the eye could see, I put two and two together. This was June 5, 1944, when the invasion forces were starting to move into position. Because of the tremendous number of aircraft required, all radar units were put on full readiness to control bombers and fighters involved in Operation Overlord. My thoughts at that time were of Madge. I wondered where she was, when she would arrive, and how I would get to greet her.

A few days later, the Red Cross informed me that Madge would arrive at 9:15 p.m. on June 10. As I walked to the station to meet her, the regular parade of buzz bombs, ack-ack fire, shelling, and aerial dogfights had commenced. When I heard a buzz bomb engine cut out, I crouched against a brick wall until I heard the explosion, and then continued. Madge arrived and looked pretty wonderful.

Our landlords, Mr. and Mrs. Legget, made a fuss about Madge and treated her like family. The next day, we planned to go to city hall to get Madge a ration book, but the Germans on the French coast began shelling. Alas, this wonderful life was too good to last, and I was shocked to learn that I was to be posted overseas. Mr. and Mrs. Legget assured me that Madge could stay with them. Once again, I bade Madge a tearful farewell.

After boarding our ship, we learned that we were going to Bombay, India. We were to become part of Combat Cargo Task Force located at Comilla in Assam. Our task was to keep the 14th Army supplied from the air with our Dakotas [transport planes]. The Task Force, which became 232 Group, RAF, South East Asia Command, carried out a continuous delivery service. Because we couldn't land, supplies were dropped down the chimney [by parachute]. We continued until March 1945, until the Japanese were on the run and the campaign came to a conclusion.

Allied strategy at this point was to organize a massive assault on the Straits of Malacca, 200 miles north of Singapore; our group, No. 232, was scheduled as supply dropper for the operation. Fortunately, this assault was not needed because the Japanese surrendered. After that, our group became an airline, flying important people on official duties.

Later, we moved to Burma, and the house we occupied there had two floors. It was dangerous to sleep on the main floor, however, because of the Burmese bandits who were killers and robbers. Consequently, we all moved upstairs and posted armed guards each night.

Finally, we got word that we were going home. In March of 1946, we were sent to Singapore. After some delay and confusion, we boarded the *King's Point Victory*, which took us to Liverpool. On May 7, 1946, I finished active service with the RAF and was reunited with Madge. I didn't need any persuasion to emigrate to Canada, and we proceeded to make the travel arrangements.

On December 7, 1946, we boarded the *Queen Elizabeth* for our journey to Canada. The crossing was very rough, and Madge, being pregnant, survived only on soda crackers and 7-Up. After we arrived in Canada, we journeyed to Kamloops, British Columbia, where I found employment as an ammunition technician at the Naval Ammunition Depot. It was a back-up for the Pacific Naval Establishment in

Esquimalt. Within three months, we had our own house and settled down to await the birth of our first child, a girl, who was born on July 1, 1946. Our son was born the next year in 1947.

With the reduction of National Defence establishments, the Kamloops Depot was closed in 1964. The City of Kamloops offered me a position as parks manager, and I worked at this job for eighteen years. My family now includes five grandchildren and seven great-grandchildren.

It has never been my desire to leave Kamloops, a city that offers all I could wish for. Sadly, Madge passed away in 2002. I am happily married to my second wife, Margaret, and pursue my great pleasure which was, and is, writing poetry. I have had two books published and two more are in the development stage. I have also been very active in the community as a volunteer. Truly, I have been blessed since leaving England.

January 2006

J.D. (Doug) Dickson

GIBSONS, BRITISH COLUMBIA

I was born in Carlisle, England, to Scottish parents. On completion of high school, I was awarded a scholarship to St. Andrews University in Scotland, my father's birthplace. There, I became an active member of the University Air Squadron and started my flying career on Tiger Moths at Leuchers in Fife. I enlisted in the RAF on April 28, 1942, and was posted to Marshall Field in Cambridge for my initial flying training, again on open-cockpit Tiger Moth biplanes. During that time, I had the misfortune to witness a German ME-109 [fighter plane] shoot down a student in a Tiger Moth ahead of me in the circuit.

After a series of courses, including an evasion and escape course at Hereford, I was posted to Canada to complete my flying training. First, it was to Bowden, Alberta, flying Cornells, and then to Penhold, Alberta, for advanced service training on Airspeed Oxfords. Having graduated high in my class, I was selected as a flying instructor and attended the Flying Instructors' School in Trenton, Ontario. Upon graduation, I was fortunate to get my preferred posting and ended up back at No. 36 SFTS in Penhold, Alberta, instructing on Airspeed Oxfords, a most gratifying occupation. It was a wonderful locale to explore Canada, with which I had fallen in love.

In general, life as a flying instructor was never boring. Correcting the potentially fatal errors of pilot trainees required

Doug and Meg Dickson on their wedding day.
(Photo: Dickson Family)

undivided attention of the instructor at all times. Little did we know that the threat could come from external sources, too.

One day, when I was teaching low flying to a student, a flash caught my eye, and I looked down to see a farmer with his shotgun aimed right at us. He was shooting as fast as he could reload. Needless to say, we took evasive action and returned to base to find pellet holes in the under part of our fuselage. The word quickly spread on the base, and we all avoided that particular farm. There were those of us who wanted to exact revenge, however. A formation of us loaded up with cases of Coke bottles, and arrived over the farm at high altitude to find the farmer outside with his shotgun. As we passed overhead, we unloaded all our bottles, which we knew from experience whistled like bombs falling. The farmer heard the crescendo and scuttled off like a rat into his drainage ditch. We never encountered any hostile fire from that farm again!

My propensity for low flying got me into serious trouble on one occasion when I had to return to base with seriously over-heated engines. The technical staff soon diagnosed the problem. The air intakes on both engines were plugged with grain, and this was a sure giveaway that I had been clipping the heads off the ripening grain fields. The chief flying instructor came up with a unique form of punishment. He offered me the choice between a court martial and the task of flying the time-expired aircraft to the wrecking yards in North Battleford. Needless to say, I chose the latter to my subsequent great regret. The aircraft were utterly decrepit and trying to get them airborne was a harrowing experience that often required bouncing over the boundary fence. After performing this task twelve times, I seriously regretted opting for that punishment instead of the court martial.

In 1944, I had just returned from a fabulous leave, having taken a cruise through the Great Lakes on the old SS *Noronic*, which later burned in Toronto Harbour. I had exhausted my entire savings and was looking forward to a very quiet weekend on base when a good friend invited me to go along on a visit to an English family who lived northwest of Edmonton in a small village called Onoway. The major attractions were a beautiful cottage on Lake St. Anne and three daughters. Being a fairly senior instructor, I was permitted to sign out an aircraft for the weekend, and I suspected that this may have been the motive behind the invitation, despite my impoverished state. After much reflection, I finally accepted the invitation with the princely sum of twenty-five cents in my pocket.

The Ledgers owned and ran a thriving general store in Onoway, and Mr. Ledger kindly met us at the airport in Edmonton and drove us the forty-five miles to their home. Apparently, we arrived earlier than expected, and we walked into their home to find the youngest daughter, Meg, with her hair all up in curlers and in her "grubby" dress. She blushed furiously and ran off to get changed and to do her hair, much to my instant interest.

That evening, when the store was closed, we all went out to their cottage at Alberta Beach. I learned that we would all be going to the dance in the local pavillion. Much to my chagrin, I learned that we had to pay ten cents for each dance, but despite my protestations and offer to pay, Meg footed the bill for the entire evening. We danced every dance together and when the music stopped, we went for a walk down the pier where we shared our first kiss under a beautiful full moon. Although it is a well-worn cliché, it was mutual love at first sight.

Our affair blossomed into a full romance, and I found my way back every weekend. There were frequent overflights and displays of aerobatics to further impress my newfound love. I visited at every opportunity, even liberating a spare aircraft on

The Avro Anson in flight.
(Photo: Commonwealth Air Training Plan Museum)

occasions for my visits, and there was the odd AWOL [absent without leave]. It became more difficult when I was posted to Pierce as an instructor at the Flying Instructors' School, but sometimes we met halfway in Calgary. By Christmas, we knew that we were hopelessly in love, and I presented Meg with a diamond ring to seal the union.

Then fate stepped in, and I was selected to go on a special mission with training at Summerside, P.E.I. At that point, we were hopelessly committed, and I asked

Meg to marry me before leaving on the mission. We tentatively set an early date, February 2, but again fate stepped in, and my course was scheduled to start on the same date. Fortunately, the staff was very understanding and gave me two weeks' leave for our honeymoon, which we happily spent in Banff, Alberta. The gods were in our corner, since the mission had tragic results, and I dodged a bullet. We were sent instead to Calgary where we found an idyllic apartment, and I continued as a wings testing officer until posted back to England.

Meg followed me to the U.K., but I could no longer settle in the confines of England after my experiences in Canada. After the war and my demobilization, we returned to Canada. Here, we have stayed ever since, and are still happily married after almost sixty-one years. We have three children, nine grandchildren and our first great-grandchild is imminent. All this started from meeting that beautiful, wonderful young lady in curlers with twenty-five cents in my pocket.

October 2005

ANDY DUNCAN

WINNIPEG, MANITOBA

I was born in Dundee, Scotland, and I joined the RAF on September 7, 1939, four days after the war started. I left Britain for Canada on November 27, 1940, my birthday, on the *Louis Pasteur*, and I was flat on my back for the entire voyage. After arriving in Halifax, about a thousand of us boarded a special train bound for No. 33 SFTS at Carberry, Manitoba, my home for the next three years. I was part of the staff in the accounting department at the base. At that time, the population of Carberry was probably about 700, and the population of the station was well over a thousand. We outnumbered the town!

It was quite a shock to see all that snow when we arrived on December 5. We got used to the cold because we were young, but sometimes the two-mile walk from the station to the town in winter seemed a little long.

As was the case with many war grooms, I met my future wife, Wilma Morris, at a dance. Even though Wilma was eighteen and a schoolteacher at the time, her widowed mother wouldn't let her go to dances because she considered her daughter to be too young. Fortunately, Wilma was able to attend one dance, only because her aunt happened to be one of the chaperones. I asked her for a dance, and things developed from there. I think we got along so well because Wilma was the only girl who could follow my lead, and we've been dancing ever since. In later years, people have commented on our dancing when we have gone on cruises.

Wilma is from Austin, Manitoba, which is about twenty-five miles from Carberry and was teaching in Harte, Manitoba. Another girl from Harte was also dating an airman from the base, and he and I would take a taxi out to Harte to see the girls. Wilma went home to Austin most weekends, and I would go there to visit her. We dated about a year before we decided to get married, and the ceremony took place in Austin United Church on July 10, 1943. I was scheduled to return to Britain shortly after, but I was hospitalized with a bad case of the flu, and my departure was postponed until December 1943. I returned on the same ship that brought me over, but the return trip was more pleasant.

I was posted to the accounting department at Charter Hall Station near Duns, which is close to the Scottish border. I was there until just before the war ended, and then I was posted to Germany where I stayed for a year-and-a-half with the Occupational Forces. I was demobilized in April 1946.

Wilma came to Britain in 1944 on the *Rangitata* along with other war brides and children. By that time, the war was winding down and it was considered safe enough to cross. Wilma's mother accepted the fact that her daughter was leaving, but she had a feeling that she would return some day.

After Wilma arrived in England, she proceeded to Edinburgh by train. There, she was supposed to get on another train which would take her to Duns. However, Wilma refused to board because her luggage was still sitting on the platform. She was told to take her luggage down to the other station at the opposite end of Waverley Street in order to catch the next train. This was to be no easy task, since no cabs were available during wartime, and suitcases did not have wheels in those days. Reluctantly, Wilma started to drag her luggage to the other station, crying all the way. A lady tram driver was driving by, and seeing that Wilma was in distress, stopped to help her. After talking to Wilma, the driver told the passengers that Wilma had recently arrived from Canada and needed their help. Some passengers got out and helped get the luggage onto the tram, and Wilma was dropped off at the next station. A few of the passengers even stayed with Wilma until her train arrived. When she didn't arrive on the first train, I was worried, but I met the second one, and there she was. To this day, Wilma has a soft spot in her heart for the Scottish

Airmen from No. 33 SFTS at a local establishment in Carberry
(Photo: Carberry Plains Archives)

The inside of an "H" hut at No. 33 SFTS.
(Photo: Commonwealth Air Training Plan Museum)

people because of this wonderful act of kindness.

At first, accommodation was not available for both of us, but Wilma was able to stay with the parents of friends we knew from Carberry. Later on, we were able to rent some rooms in a private home, although the landlady did the cooking for us.

Wilma enjoyed her four years in Britain, and our son was born there in 1947. Why did we return to Canada? Well, I loved to travel, and I had enjoyed my time in Canada. I felt that in the long term, Wilma would not be happy spending her entire life in Britain. I didn't need much persuasion to emigrate, however. By that time, my mother had died and my father had remarried. I had been away from home for seven years because of my war service, and my family ties weren't strong.

We almost settled in Toronto. I was supposed to have a job interview there, but because I couldn't find the place, we got back on the train and came to Winnipeg. After working for a few companies, I got a good job with the City of St. James as the treasurer. When St. James amalgamated to form Metro Winnipeg and then the City of Winnipeg, I became the budget director. I retired from that job in 1984.

I have no regrets about coming to Canada. It's been great! The cold in the winter and the heat in the summer have never bothered me. We have two children and two grandchildren. Both our grandchildren are unmarried, so we have no great-grandchildren yet.

September 2005

CYRIL FOSH

WINNIPEG, MANITOBA

I was born in Barking, Essex, England. I was posted to Canada in 1943, and I spent much of my time in Moose Jaw, Saskatchewan, as a flying instructor, although I was in Carberry, Manitoba, for a while. I enjoyed my time as a flying instructor, although there were a few times when I almost preferred to face the German Luftwaffe rather than take some of those pilot trainees up in an aircraft. Most of the boys took to flying well, but there were a few of them who would panic. Instructing required constant vigilance.

I met my future wife, Fay Hatch, while I was on leave in Winnipeg. She was with a group of girls, and I was with my air force friends. We met in a book store, of all places. Both groups got to talking as young people do, and I asked Fay to a dance that was coming up. I wasn't much of a dancer, but neither was Fay, and that suited us both. We attempted only the slow dances. Fay was working at J.C. Wilson Ltd., and I tried to impress her by flying my plane low over the building where she worked. I did that about three times before Fay told me to stop. I was becoming an embarrassment.

I proposed to Fay with the classic question, "Will you marry me?" It wasn't the most original proposal in the world, but it worked. Fay's parents were supportive and approved of the marriage. They thought I was a sensible young man, although I'm sure they didn't know that I buzzed Fay's workplace.

After we became engaged, I was posted to Ottawa. Fay was able to travel to Ottawa by train, and that's where we were married in the fall of 1943. I was later posted to the east coast of Canada, and we lived in that region for a while. The crunch finally came, as we knew it would, and I was posted to the U.K. We made the necessary arrangements, and Fay was able to get passage to Britain. Fay said good-bye to her parents at the train station, and her mother shed a few tears. It was a sad time for her parents, but Fay was determined to join me in England.

Some time after Fay's arrival, I learned that I was to be posted to northern India to train Indian pilots. Fay was three months' pregnant when I heard about my posting to India, and I wanted her to be sent back to Canada to be out of harm's way while I was gone. If she had stayed, she would have had to live in London with my family, and the area where they lived was often bombed. I didn't want her to have to go through all that. When I approached the Air Ministry about my request, I was told that returning to Canada wasn't part of the deal when we made the application for Fay to come to Britain. I informed the Air Ministry that I was going to sit on their steps, and I wasn't going to leave until they changed their minds. They relented, and Fay returned to the safety of Canada while I was in India.

The war finally ended, and I was sent back to the U.K., where I was demobilized. When I left India, I took with me a carpet that measured five feet by seven feet. How I managed to lug that thing around, I don't know. We had it for several years before it wore out.

I had always wanted to come to Canada, and I knew that was where my future lay. After I got here, I decided to start my own business. Before the war, I had worked as a sign painter in England, and I had some experience in this field. I went out and got orders for signs from businesses in Winnipeg, and I sat down at my mother-in-law's kitchen table to paint. The rest is history. My business was called Fosh Signs and Displays Limited, and I ran it with several employees until I retired. I have no regrets about leaving England, although we did go back for a few visits. After I retired, we travelled a lot, and we have visited Australia, New Zealand, South Africa, and Hawaii. Out of six brothers and two sisters, I have only one sister left in England. We have four children and seven grandchildren to date.

It's hard for us to remember all these events that happened so long ago. Fay is eighty-three and I'm eighty-eight. We can hardly remember what we had for breakfast, never mind the events that happened more than sixty years ago.

October 2005

No. 33 SFTS at Carberry, Manitoba, hosted many VIPs, including the Duke of Kent, seen in the picture above. (Photo: Commonwealth Air Training Plan Museum)

WILLIAM (BILL) GILES

BRIDGEWATER, NOVA SCOTIA

I was born on August 31, 1920, in Lancaster, England, the fourth and last child in my family. My married sister was in Burma, and my brothers were sixteen and fourteen when I came along. Needless to say, I had a wonderful childhood, although I was very spoiled.

I was attending Storey's Technical Institute on a scholarship when war with Germany was declared. Having heard many horror stories from my older pals who had been drafted into the army, I volunteered for the Royal Air Force Volunteer Reserve, and I was called up in April of 1940. I was told that flight mechanics were badly needed, and that I could later transfer to aircrew. Ha! Ha! I certainly fell for that line.

I left England in April 1941, bound for Canada. I was destined to become a very small part of the British Commonwealth Air Training Plan. Because the *Bismarck* [German battleship] was on the prowl, our ship, the *Royal Ulsterman*, was diverted to Iceland where we stayed for a few days. We then boarded a small liner called the *Circassia*, which had been taken over by the Royal Navy. There were about twenty or thirty of us RAF bods on board, and we were just like tourists. The sailors told us that our ship was sailing through icefields to avoid the German battleship that had sunk the *Hood*. We laughed and told them that nothing could sink the *Hood*. After we landed in Halifax and boarded a train for Debert, Nova Scotia, we learned that what the sailors had told us was true.

When we arrived at No. 31 OTU in Debert, it was

Bill and Ella Giles on their wedding day.
(Photo: Giles Family)

still under construction. The runways were unpaved, and there was not an airplane in sight. There was nothing to do at this stage, and we had a ball. Most of my RAF service was with Training Command, and I helped to service the planes that were used for training. Although I was not classified as aircrew, I did a lot of flying because of air and engine tests.

I was brought up to believe that England was the centre of the universe. The house where I was born and raised was of solid stone construction and was built in the 1600s. In England, "central heating" meant having a fireplace that burned coal. Consequently, everybody shivered and shook indoors during the winter in the U.K. It was a different story in Canada, however. The Clark home where I stayed on my weekend off before I met Ella had a pipeless furnace with a big register in the middle of the hallway. When I stood over that and felt the wonderful heat, I thought, "My God, these colonials have it over us."

As for my love life, I was on a weekend pass in October 1941 and was staying at the Clark home in Windsor, Nova Scotia. The good people of Windsor had fixed up an empty store on the main street as a comfort club for servicemen. I was there when this good-looking girl came around with a plate of sandwiches, my favourite food. We hit it off right away, and I walked her home after she got off duty at nine o'clock. It's hard to believe now, but I was so disoriented after meeting Ella and walking her home, that I had a hard time finding the place where I was billeted. When I finally arrived, the lady of the house was quite concerned because my buddy had got there ahead of me. After a thorough grilling about my tardiness, the lady of the house deduced that the girl in question was Ella Cochrane, a schoolteacher who came from a prominent and respected family in Windsor. On subsequent leaves, I became a regular guest in the Cochrane home.

About Christmas 1942, I learned that I was to be posted to England. At that point, Ella and I were hopelessly in love. During my Christmas leave, we decided to get married, and Ella's family was very gracious about it. Because Ella's family was Baptist, we were married by their minister in the family home. The only two people present, other than the family, were Len and Helen Tunnah who lived across the street. Helen and Ella had been friends over the years.

I returned to duty and reported that I was married. Because of my newly acquired marital status, I missed the overseas draft and was transferred to No. 36 Operational Training Unit Greenwood, just down the valley from Windsor. Marvellous! My family was a little shocked when they found out that I was married. They were High Anglican and were a little chagrined when they learned that I married outside their faith. They came, however, to love Ella as a member of the family and looked forward to her visits after the war.

Eventually, all good things come to an end, and I was sent to the U.K. While in England, I was stationed at Tholthorpe with No. 6 Group RCAF before being posted in October 1944 to No. 148 Squadron RAF in Brindisi, Italy. Although the No. 148 was listed as a bomber squadron, it was actually a special squadron that dropped supplies to the partisans in Yugoslavia and Greece. We had Winston Churchill's son, Randolph, with us for a while. He would be parachuted in to set up the rendezvous for the drops.

When I first joined the squadron, we were using Halifaxes with Merlin engines. On the ill-fated operation to drop supplies to the partisans in Danzig, we lost all the planes, and we were later supplied with Liberators. The squadron then moved from Brindisi to Foggia, Italy, where we shared the airfield with Americans, a very pleasant experience.

When the war ended in Europe, the whole squadron flew over to Ginaclis in Egypt and got set up to be a staging post to ferry troops from Europe to the war in Asia. We were all set to go when the war with Japan ended.

I came back to England in March 1946 and was released by the RAF, but not discharged. The Canadian government would not allow me to come to Canada until I was discharged. The RAF would not discharge me until I had official permission to enter Canada. In August, the problem was resolved. I knew that Canada was where I wanted to spend the rest of my life.

I came to Canada on the *Mauritania* in August of 1946 as a landed immigrant. Two weeks later, I went to work for Stedman Brothers' Department Store in Windsor. Then, in January 1948, I became the manager of the store in Bridgewater. Subsequently, I learned that there was a vacancy for a customs officer working out of the Windsor Port. I was fortunate to be appointed and served for thirty-two years, first as a boarding officer. Later, I became the registrar of shipping and then, the collector of customs and excise. I retired as a customs inspector. Canada is the greatest country in the world, and I am proud to have been a citizen since 1952.

It's strange what one remembers as the years go by. I met Ella many years ago when she was serving me sandwiches in Windsor. After we were married, she would often ask me if I wanted a lunch before we went to bed, and I usually said that I wouldn't mind a sandwich. On one occasion when Ella served me a sandwich, she remarked, "You know, Bill, I met you serving sandwiches, and I have been serving them to you ever since."

Ella and I were married for more than forty-four years, and we had no children. However, Ella had two brothers in Windsor whose children brought us much joy over the years. When Ella died in 1987, I was devastated. Helen Tunnah, our good friend, had lost her husband, Len, ten years earlier. She and I started to see each other, and we were married a year later. Sadly, I lost Helen two years ago. I am very fortunate to have had the love and companionship of two wonderful women. Helen and Len had three children, who are now mine and treat me as family. Because of Helen and Len, I have become a father, grandfather and great-grandfather, and I am very proud of that. Who could ask for more?

I have been most fortunate.

August 2006

Norman James (Ginger) Hailes

WINNIPEG, MANITOBA

Both Norman and Christine have passed away. The following story was submitted by their daughter, Wendy Gray.

Norman James Hailes was born on November 1, 1921, in Gloucester, England. He was called "Ginger" because of his red hair, and the name stuck with him throughout his life. He was one of a family of eight children—three boys and five girls. As a child, my father spent much of his time getting into mischief and being at odds with his mother's disciplinary actions. When he was very young, my dad would often take his father's lunch pail to him at the Gloucester Oil Mills where he was employed.

Dad joined the RAF when he was seventeen. According to my aunt in England, he had a girlfriend at the time, but his parents did not approve of the relationship. The problem was solved by the RAF when Dad was posted overseas to an unknown place called Carberry, Manitoba. He was part of the operational staff and serviced the engines on the training aircraft. Before he enlisted, Dad had worked in a garage and enjoyed this line of work immensely.

Dad was impressed by the friendliness and the hospitality of the people in Carberry who opened their homes to the young airmen. My grandparents did their part, too, and often invited airmen to their home. That is how their daughter,

Ginger and Christine Hailes on their wedding day.
(Photo: Wendy Gray)

Christine Elizabeth Baron, first met my father. I don't believe it was "love at first sight," because there was another young man in my mother's life at the time, but their paths would eventually cross again

The citizens of Carberry organized many social events for the airmen and the young people in the community, and my parents took part in many of the activities. On one such occasion, when my father and mother were out with a group of young people, my mother tripped and fell, and Dad tried to help her up. My mother told him emphatically that she was perfectly capable of getting up herself. Those inauspicious circumstances were the beginnings of a courtship, an engagement, and a marriage. Neither of their families was keen on wartime marriages, especially since both of my parents were so young at the time. In spite of many objections, Mom and Dad were married on December 16, 1941, in the United Church in Carberry. My oldest brother, Norman Thomas John, was born in Carberry on August 24, 1942. The baby was sick and could not tolerate the milk. There were no special formulas in those days, and my mother didn't know what to do with him. It was a real worry for her.

After Dad was posted to the U.K. in 1944, Mom had to cope on her own with the limited allowance from his British wages. It was difficult trying to make ends meet, but she persevered with the help from her family.

After Dad was released from the RAF, he tried to arrange passage to Canada, but it took several months. He had enjoyed his time in Carberry and had no hesitation about making a permanent home in Canada. After Dad returned to his Canadian family, he became a carpenter, a skill he learned from his grandfather and great-grandfather. However, he missed military life and decided to enlist in the RCAF, becoming an aero engine technician.

Dad was very gifted mechanically. He could repair anything and spent many happy hours tinkering and inventing. He even took out a patent on one of his inventions. I remember the time when Dad invented his own power plant because he hated paying the electricity bill. It actually worked quite well after he got the bugs out.

During the time Dad was in the RCAF, our family lived on the base in Rivers and in Germany. To get to the base in Germany, we made the journey on the SS *Atlantic*. Although I was very young at the time, I remember many details about that trip, even our cabin numbers. The trip stood out in my mother's memory, too, because she broke her tooth on that crossing. We stayed with my grandparents in Gloucester, England, for a while because the base in Germany was not quite ready for families. After the posting in Germany was completed, we were fortunate to be able to fly home, thus avoiding another ocean voyage. The air flight home was not without incident, however. I was airsick, and I

The grounds at No. 33 SFTS. Carberry, Manitoba, can be seen in the background.
(Photo: Commonwealth Air Training Plan Museum)

upchucked all over Dad's brand new uniform.

It seems that the little incidents in life stand out in one's memory. I remember the times when Dad would drive us out to the base to let us watch the planes take off and land. On another occasion when I was very young, Dad took me out to the hangar where he worked. I climbed onto a chair and looked out the window. I saw Dad chalking the wheels of a little yellow plane with wooden wedges to keep it from rolling away. I doubled over in laughter when I was told that the plane was called a Chipmunk.

After Dad was released from the RCAF, he worked as a park attendant in Rivers Park in Rivers, Manitoba. He loved the outdoors, and he impressed us with his knowledge of plants and animals. My siblings and I used to walk to the park with our lunches to be with Dad, and then we would all walk home together. Mom enjoyed these outings, too, because we were out of her hair for a while. The seedlings that Dad planted when he was a park attendant are now fully grown.

Dad's true calling was mechanics, however, and it was the occupation he returned to after being a park attendant. Although his military days were over, he was employed as a civilian at the Canadian Forces Base in Rivers. There, he worked in the Heavy Equipment Maintenance Department. When that base closed, he was transferred to Camp Shilo, and he continued to work there until he retired.

My parents were divorced in 1983, and we weren't surprised. Not all wartime marriages worked out, and we realized that it was for the best. After the divorce, Mom lived in Brandon where she died in 1989 of congestive heart failure. She is buried in the family plot in Carberry Cemetery. Dad later remarried and moved to Winnipeg. Unfortunately, Dad was killed in an accident on October 10, 1997. He was riding one of those scooters that many older people use to get around, and when he was crossing a street, he was hit by a truck. We were all shaken by this senseless tragedy.

My parents had eight children—three boys and five girls. Ironically, Dad came from a family of exactly the same size and gender proportion. As one can imagine, there are several grandchildren descended from that family of eight, including my own children.

Wendy Gray, September 2006

JOHN HALL

STRATFORD, ONTARIO

John Hall passed away on June 28, 2005, at the age of eighty-six. His widow, Jean, sent me his brief memoirs which he had written in 1999.

Four score years ago, at nearly Christmastime, I came into this world at approximately 1:30 p.m. It was a Monday. I was born into a wonderful family of five girls and two boys. There were also twin boys and another brother who all died in the epidemics. I well remember one Christmas. My dad went to the dump and found my Christmas present. It was a magic lantern, and to me it really was magic. One had to put a candle in it to show the glass slides on the walls.

With a family of seven children during hard times, many of our presents were

John and Jean Hall on their wedding day.
(Photo: Hall Family)

either hand-me-downs or homemade. I can still remember the Depression, although like many other children at that time, I cannot remember some of the incidents that must have been devastating to our parents. I found out later. I do remember the man who used to come around our village early every morning to wake us. He tapped on the bedroom windows to "knock us up," a popular phrase in that part of Britain. This phrase has a different meaning in England. He used a long pole with some cloth on the end so as not to break the windows. I also remember hearing the town crier's booming voice when King George V died.

About school, well, that was another kettle of fish! I apparently went backwards instead of forward. It was not until 1937 when I joined the RAF that I returned to school. I liked the Service. I remember flying in the biplanes and literally hanging by the seat of my pants, strapped in only with a steel wire and firing my gun at the drogue [target] pulled by another plane. It was all on film, and we could see if we had hit the drogue.

I came to Canada in January 1941 when the temperature was forty-two below zero and was sent back to England on December 6, 1943. During my time in Canada, I found myself a girl at one of the camp dances. I married her on April 25, 1942, and we have been together ever since. We had a double wedding in Brandon with my wife's friend and her RAF corporal.

I have many memories of my time at Carberry [No. 33 SFTS]. I remember once making a really silly mistake. I took off my gauntlets at forty degrees below zero while starting a Model 1 Harvard, and was taken to the hospital with the handle frozen to my hand. The groundcrew had to partly disassemble the plane in order to rescue me. I remember the hot summer in Carberry when the grass snakes were inches deep on the roads. Another time, we saw a cloud of locusts, and we all thought that a storm was coming. The locusts landed and ate the canvas off the planes, all seventy-two of them. Then they ate all the leaves off the trees.

[After the war, I received my discharge from the RAF], and I returned to Canada on March 6, 1946. I looked for a job, and within one week, I had one with the CNR at the car yards in Transcona, Manitoba. I really liked my job and never had one sick day.

In 1954, I joined the Canadian Army. I served for fifteen years with the RCAMC [Medical Corps]. When I was posted to Churchill, Manitoba, I had many interesting experiences, such as whaling on Hudson Bay, constructing an igloo (I spent the night in it), and taking Boy Scouts out onto the tundra all fastened together with a rope. We didn't want to lose anyone in the whiteouts. I also remember being chased by a polar bear. While in Churchill, I built a lovely baby crib and shipped it to Winnipeg for our six-week-old daughter. I also helped to build floats for a parade while I was there.

In 1968, after my discharge from the Army, I started work with the ambulance service in Stratford, Ontario. I was an ambulance supervisor, but I also had management duties and other responsibilities in the hospital. I retired in January 1984 after almost sixteen years.

I have achieved many of my boyhood dreams. I went down in a submarine and up in an aircraft and a balloon. I also visited Adolph Hitler's retreat in Berchesgaden, Germany, and I toured King Ludwig's castle in Bavaria.

Jean Hall added these words to her late husband's memoirs:

My memories take me back to 1940–41. I was working for the T. Eaton Company in Brandon and was boarding at the home of my girlfriend, whom we called "Bubbles." On Saturday nights, chaperoned dances were held at the Armouries for service personnel, and local girls received invitations. Bubbles and I enjoyed these dances because we had a chance to meet many nice young men. Bubbles and I seemed to take to the RAF chaps (she called them "blokes") with their baggy old uniforms and their various accents. In June 1941, Bubbles and I met our future husbands. After a courtship of six months, all four of us became engaged at Christmas. We had a double wedding ceremony on April 25, 1942.[6]

John and I began our lives together as happy newlyweds. Our first home was in Brandon in a private home. It was one room with kitchen privileges, a pump for water and outdoor plumbing. John came home weekends. By fall, John had found two rooms in a house in Carberry, and we gathered up our bits and pieces and moved there. I wasn't much of a cook then, but became quite adept with a can opener if all else failed. My lessons in "keeping the home fires burning" were about to begin. I was to learn how to chop wood and kindling and carry out the ashes that go with the job. We had two rooms, one up and one down, and the heat never made it to the second floor. One thing we did have was a big, six-foot-long kitchen table. Our friends from across the hall, Cyril and Gwen Brooker, asked if they might borrow our table because the doctor was coming that afternoon to pull out Gwen's teeth. They needed an operating table. We got our water from the pump in the shed, when it was not frozen.

We were to move again up the street to another two rooms in a private house with all the trimmings which included a pump, outdoor plumbing, and a big old cook stove that provided another chance to keep the home fires burning. Our son was born there, delivered by a very kind Scottish midwife because the doctor was out of town on a call. The baby was premature and was kept alive for the first week of his life on the oven door. There was no hospital and, of course, no incubator. My knuckles were soon to discover the scrub board. There were no disposable diapers in those days. The landlady began to complain that the baby's crying was upsetting

---

[6] See Tom Brock's story.

the household, and that we were using too much electricity.

Consequently, we moved to another house up the street; not a wise choice as we were soon to discover. It was a big, rambling house made into apartments to accommodate the married military personnel. We had one room with a big bruiser of a cook stove that belched out black smoke every time it was lit, a pump in the shed, outdoor plumbing, and rats, an added bonus! It was quite terrifying, especially at night, so we kept the lights on. We set traps for them, but they kept coming. After we returned from a week's leave in Winnipeg, we found that the rats had left a nest made from old newspapers in the baby's crib and had chewed the binding on the flannelette crib sheets.

We decided that enough was enough, and the baby and I returned to Winnipeg to be near my family. John visited us as often as he could. My sister, whose husband was overseas, found me an attic room in the rooming house where she lived. Once again, I was keeping the home fires burning, but this time I was feeding quarters into a gas meter so that the baby and I could keep warm with a two-burner gas stove.

On December 6, 1943, John was sent back to England, just when our five-month old baby was very sick, and I was pregnant. I had the opportunity to move into a rented house with my elderly parents, and they were good to me, but money was short. They had only their old age pensions, which were about $40 at the time. I was in dire straits, too, because I was put on the British allowance of $60 a month for some time. Fortunately, my mother knew 1,001 ways of turning leftovers into

The grounds at No. 33 SFTS.
(Photo: Commonwealth Air Training Plan Museum)

gourmet meals and just about as many ways to stretch a dollar. A daughter was born in June 1944. My father spent much of the time in his rocking chair, singing to the little ones and telling them stories. He wore out his rocking chair after two years.

Mail, parcels and snapshots were very important during the war, and the lady who owned the corner store put aside various treats which I sent to John. I well remember one parcel I sent to John's family. It was returned for re-packaging, a greasy, soggy mess. I had sent butter that had leaked out.

Most afternoons I took the children for an airing in the pram, and one particular afternoon as I passed Pratt Hardware on Portage Avenue, I spotted a lovely English bone-china tea set for $7.95. Like a child looking into a toy store window, I felt I just had to have it, but I knew our budget didn't allow for any extravagances. Each day, I walked by to see if the set was still there. One day, with my money clutched in my hand, I went in and bought it. I was so proud of that set, and it was well used.

The war ended and life continued. In March 1946, my husband returned to his Canadian family. My children were too young to know who this stranger was, but in time, things worked out. In 1947 another son was born, and we were then in our wartime house. We were in seventh heaven, in spite of the mud. There were no roads, no sidewalks, and no landscaping. It rained and rained, and neither the postman nor the milkman could get within two blocks of us.

We raised our four children—David, Janice, Murray and Brenda—and we survived twenty-four moves. My loving husband died on June 28, 2005, and the funeral was held in Stratford, Ontario. The internment of ashes was at Chapel Lawn Cemetery in Winnipeg on September 23, 2005. John was buried alongside his eldest son, David, who died in September 1988. Our friends, Bubbles and Tom Brock, who shared our double wedding ceremony, are still going strong and live in Ottawa.

Jean Hall, December 2005

Doug Harrington

HAMILTON, ONTARIO

I lived in the County of Surrey in England, and I joined the RAF in August of 1941. Prior to that, I had been working for a company that manufactured aircraft instruments. After some delay, I reported for duty and spent many months at various locations carrying out preliminary aircrew training. In October 1942, I boarded the *Queen Elizabeth* and ended up a week later in New York City. Our draft then boarded a train that deposited us at Moncton, New Brunswick. This was a personnel depot for all trainees entering or leaving Canada or the United States.

From time to time, groups of trainees were posted away to various training stations in Canada or the U.S. Eventually, I was posted to No. 6 Bombing and Gunnery School, RCAF Station, Mountain View, Ontario, and arrived there in January 1943. The winter of 1942–43 was bitterly cold in Ontario, and the airmen from the U.K. had experienced nothing like it before. Much of our training took place outside, firing the guns. The ground training classes and the flying training were co-ordinated so that we put into practice in the air what we had hopefully learned on the ground. All bombing and gunnery exercises took place over Lake Ontario. We wrote our exams and, by mid-March, we had finished and were ready for the next portion of our training, which would be a concentrated, five-month course in air navigation. The orders arrived, and we found ourselves on board the train headed for No. 8 Air Observer School, a few miles outside Quebec City

The training at Ancienne Lorette was to last twenty weeks, and it followed the familiar format of co-ordinated ground school and flying. We had most weekends free and always gravitated into town for movies, dances, etc. The Beaver Restaurant was a favourite hangout for my friends and me. Apparently, we were seen there by Margaret White and her friend on one occasion, but I was unaware of it at the time. A week or so later, another airman and I were strolling along Dufferin Terrace alongside the Château Frontenac which overlooked the St. Lawrence River. This spot was a well known location for meeting the local girls, and we accosted, if that's the right word, two attractive girls with the lame line, "Haven't we met before?"

To my surprise, the answer was, "Yes," and Margaret told me that she had seen me in the Beaver Restaurant the week before. At that time, I had shaken my head in reply to something said by one of my buddies, and she had turned to her friend and whispered, "He may be shaking his head now, but one day, he's going to mean something to me." This story was not told to me at the time, but considerably later.

From this inauspicious beginning, I spent a great deal of my remaining time in Ancienne Lorette with Margaret White. I was welcomed into her home, met her parents, went dancing with her, and generally enjoyed her company. She and her sister came to my wings parade in late July. Later, I spent a leave in the States, followed by a posting to Summerside, Prince Edward Island. After that, I was posted to Nassau, Bahamas, and then to Dorval, Quebec. I managed trips to Quebec City after Nassau, but they were of short duration. The crunch came in March of 1944. I was due to ferry an aircraft from Dorval to Scotland, and my romantic affair in Quebec seemingly came to an end.

Once I left Quebec City, Margaret and I started corresponding by mail, and once I arrived back in the U.K., we were each keeping our respective post offices busy with three or more letters per week. Because of censorship, I could say little of what I was doing, but she was able to fill me in on her nursing studies at

Doug and Margaret Harrington on their wedding day. (Photo: Harrington Family)

a Quebec City hospital. Our correspondence continued hot and heavy while I was in England, and then in September 1944, my squadron was sent to Iceland.

Exactly what it was about Iceland, I'm not sure. Maybe it was the horrible weather, or the sense of isolation, or whatever, but in February 1945 I actually proposed marriage by letter! It took a while to get an answer, and I was on tenterhooks. When the answer finally came, it was a big "YES." There was no "down on the knees," no ring, no celebration, nothing!

Our letter-writing continued for the rest of the war. I was released from service in 1946, and Margaret qualified as a registered nurse the same year. My intention was to return to Canada, but I was frustrated by the complete lack of transportation in a westerly direction. Eventually, Margaret managed to get a passage to England in June 1947, and we were married there in August the same year. We both worked for the next three years, and then, in June 1950, Margaret returned to visit her family. While she was away, I took the plunge and arrived in Canada in September 1950. Here we are in 2005 and fifty-eight years later! You'd have to say it was a resounding success.

December 2005

KEN HARRIS

VICTORIA, BRITISH COLUMBIA

In 1942, my husband, Ken Harris, came to Canada with the RAF as part of the BCATP, and was stationed at No. 33 SFTS in Carberry, Manitoba. When he first arrived, he was part of the groundcrew, but later, he re-mustered as an air gunner.

My maiden name was Kathleen Downey. Like many other couples, Ken and I met at a dance at the Recreation Centre at the base. Invitations were sent out to all the single girls in the area. These dances were all well-chaperoned, but for all that, Dad was reluctant to let my sister and me go. He eventually relented, thank goodness, and allowed us to attend the dance. Can you imagine all those naïve, country girls entering a hall to find a long line of young airmen waiting to greet them? Add to that, the English custom to get your hand kissed as a greeting. We were all taken back by this gesture, and we were embarrassed, for our hands were pretty rough and work-worn. Many of the girls were needed on the farms, especially when so many of the boys were in the Service.

If you didn't know the modern dances, you learned in short order. Some of the airmen were good singers, and so, we sang as we danced. It was such an exciting time to be a young girl!

Most times, there would be lads staying with us on leave for the weekend. They didn't get much pay, and most families would invite airmen to their homes. On Sunday nights, the lads could go to the Carberry Recreation Centre where they could sing and treats would be served. Many were still teenagers, and most of them were away from home for the first time. The Carberry folk adopted them, more or less, and the doors were always open to them.

Ken and Kathleen Harris (left) on their wedding day. (Photo: Harris Family)

Many of the boys were very talented. Some of them formed a group called The Ripchords and they put on fantastic musical shows. They were a big hit in Winnipeg, too. Ken was also talented, and he loved to play the harmonica.

When the base first opened, the airmen would venture into the local beer parlour. At first, some of the old-timers got annoyed because the airmen would start singing in the beer parlour. The boys were upsetting their routine. However, one gentleman said, "Look at it this way. If they're singing, they aren't fighting and getting into trouble." In time, the locals got used to it and, I expect, quite enjoyed it.

After Ken volunteered to re-muster as an air gunner, he was transferred to the school at Macdonald, Manitoba, just outside of Portage la Prairie. He was stationed there for just over three months and received a commission when he graduated.

During his time at Carberry and at Macdonald, Ken and I saw each other often, and he was a regular guest in my family's home. He just seemed to fit in it so easily. We both knew that the time would come when we would have to say our final good-byes, but we tried not to think about it too much. I knew what was in store for Ken when he was posted to active duty. We were not to meet again for many years. While Ken was away, we exchanged hundreds of letters.

As time went on, Ken received promotions and became a flight lieutenant before he was finally discharged. Promotions came fast during wartime. He flew in the following aircraft: Halifaxes, Ansons, Martinets, DC3s, and Marauders. Many of his

Carberry Boat Song performed by the Ripchords at one of their many concerts.
(Photo: Carberry Plains Archives)

The Ripchords during rehearsal. This talented group of airmen from No. 33 performed in many concerts, not only in Carberry, but also at several other locations.
(Photo: Carberry Plains Archive)

operational flights took place over Germany, but he was also in Italy. At one time, he was stationed in South Africa with No. 12 Squadron. He was one of the fortunate ones to survive. Many of his friends weren't so fortunate.

In 1944, a call came out to help in a munitions factory in Toronto. My oldest sister, Irene, was married to an airman in the RCAF who was overseas. She and I volunteered to work in the factory making anti-aircraft shells. I really enjoyed playing a part in the war effort. I recall that there were a number of girls from Western Canada who volunteered to work in this plant. We went by train to Toronto, and it was the first time many of us slept in a berth. It was an exciting experience, and friendships were formed which lasted for many years. We did visit Niagara Falls and two aunts before going home. It was a happy day when peace was declared.

Of course, lots of letter-writing went on during this time, and I wrote to many of our boys overseas, including Ken. I wrote to family members and the sons of neighbours, and I recall that I sent off more than thirty letters every month. Most of us tried to do our bit to keep up the spirits of all the boys overseas, and we made sure that our letters were cheery and newsy.

After the war, I spent a number of years in Winnipeg, working first at the university and then in a medical clinic. After the war and his discharge, Ken stayed in England to care for his mother who had cancer. During all the years that Ken was in England, we corresponded regularly, and that is how we sustained our relationship. After his mother passed away, Ken worked hard to save money as fast as possible. He had always intended to return to Canada, but needed a sponsor, however, and my parents agreed to sponsor him.

Ken came to Canada in 1954, but jobs were scarce at that time. He helped out on the farm at first, but then he got a job as a machinist. When that job ended, he decided to join the RCAF. The pay was poor, but the benefits were good. He chose to become a transport driver, as it was the shortest course offered.

In January 1955, Ken and I were married in my parents' home. It was a lovely wedding. Family members and neighbours all pitched in and helped with the decorating and the reception. The next day was my parents' anniversary, and there was another grand party.

The Ripchords after a performance.
(Photo: Carberry Plains Archive)

We had a few days together in Winnipeg before Ken was off to Edmonton, and I went back to work. I followed about two weeks later. We stayed in Edmonton for four years, and two of our boys were born there. Then, it was off to France for four years where our third son was born. Our last posting was in Southport, Manitoba, and we were able to drive home to Carberry often to see my family.

In 1969, Ken reached his fiftieth birthday, and his air force days were over. Before he retired, he had been to the West Coast on a military trip and, of course, being an Englishman, he fell in love with Victoria. To make a long story short, the Harris family packed up their three boys and their belongings once school was over and headed west. Times were tough, but we've never been sorry we chose Victoria. Ken's final retirement came in 1984, and two years later, he died. Before he passed away that year, we did fly to England and had a good visit with Charlie Brown, his buddy from his RAF days in Carberry.

In 1990, I remarried, and every year, Mick, my second husband, my sister Hazel from Kelowna, and I would drive home to Carberry. Mick passed away in 1997, so Hazel and I now fly home and will continue to do so as long we are able.

Incidentally, my sister, Hazel Hopton, also married an airman from Britain.[7]

Kathleen Harris Maguire, November 2005

---

[7] See Leslie Hopton's story.

JOHN HAYBALL

CARBERRY, MANITOBA

My husband, John Hayball, was born in London, England. He was in the RAF and was sent to Canada in December 1940 on the *Louis Pasteur*. John and his friends had no idea where they were destined, and everyone thought that they were bound for India. The ship broke down on the voyage across the Atlantic, and the convoy had to leave them behind. Being stranded in U-boat waters was extremely dangerous, especially at that stage of the war. Apparently, the British crew on this French ship didn't fully understand how to operate it, and the repairs took some time to complete. Eventually, the ship got underway. As the ship approached Halifax, RCAF planes were sent out to escort the *Louis Pasteur* into port. Years later, when neighbours came over to our cottage at Clear Lake in Riding Mountain National Park, the men would talk about their war experiences. As it turned out, Jack Barker, our neighbour, was the pilot of one of the planes sent out to escort the *Louis Pasteur* into port.

John and Rowena Hayball in their later years. (Photo: Hayball Family)

During the passage, many of the airmen were seasick. Before the voyage, one of John's friends bragged that he had a strong stomach and would never be seasick. Nevertheless, he lost his false teeth as he leaned over the rail to throw up.

John was in Signals [communication] and was stationed at No. 33 SFTS in Carberry, Manitoba. At that time, I was a telephone operator for the town, and because of our jobs, John and I had talked on the phone a few times. Eventually, we agreed to meet at a dance where my mother was one of the chaperones. Many of the local families would invite the airmen over for dinner, and my mother invited John, never realizing what was in store. John and I started dating, but my mother never approved of the relationship. She was afraid that John would take me away to live in England, and she didn't want to lose me. She had only two children, and my brother was in the army. She continuously tried to find fault with John, and made comments such as, "He's too skinny."

John and I wanted to get married, and because of the situation with my mother, we decided to elope. I took the bus to Portage la Prairie, and my girlfriend drove John there in her car. We were married in the Presbyterian min-

*John and Rowena Hayball
shortly after they were married.*
(Photo: Hayball Family)

ister's residence on August 31, 1941. I was nineteen and John was twenty-eight. We spent our wedding night at another girlfriend's home in Portage la Prairie. When my mother found out what had happened, she told us to come home, and she resigned herself to the situation.

My father and brother were supportive. My father was the local butcher in Carberry, and I overheard one of his customers ask him why he let me marry an Englishman. My father said that it was up to me to choose the man I wanted, and that made me feel really good.

As time went on, my mother came to love John. He always told her that no one could cook like her, and she never tired of hearing that. There was an empty suite above my father's shop, and John and I lived there for a time, although we were able to rent a cottage for six months. My son was born on May 22, 1943. After John was transferred to England, I put our furniture into storage and moved back with my family.

During the war, John was in France, Belgium, Holland and Germany working in Signals from a truck. He and other airmen followed the troops across Europe, and usually operated very close to the front lines. They would set up wires with tin cans around the truck so that they could be warned if the enemy tried to sneak up on them. Once in a while, an officer would forget about the wire, and the noise would cause all of them to reach for their guns. John told me that everyone's nerves were strained after months of this kind of work.

After John was demobilized in 1946, he came to Canada. He had come to love

Canada, and he had no regrets about leaving England. He became a Canadian in 1967 and was very proud of his citizenship. He loved living in Carberry where he knew everybody. He liked people, and the feeling was mutual. Small-town life really agreed with him.

John's first job was with North American Lumber in Carberry. In 1954, he was transferred to Meacham, Saskatchewan, and by that time, we had a daughter. After that, he was transferred again, this time to Lipton, Saskatchewan, which was not far from Regina. In 1962, we moved back to Carberry, and John worked for the provincial government in highways until he retired. Sadly, John died in 2001 of Alzheimer's disease, and spent the last few years of his life in the care home in Carberry. His last few years were very hard on the family.

I was let go from my job as a telephone operator as soon as I got married. Married women weren't allowed to work for the telephones in those days. Because there was a shortage of labour during the war, I was called back and worked on a casual basis in Carberry. When we lived in Saskatchewan, I got a job as a telephone operator there. After we returned to Carberry, I was re-hired and became the head operator, a job I held until 1977. When dial-up phones came in, I was transferred to Brandon, and I worked there until I retired in 1983.

We had two children, two grandchildren and one great-grandchild. John loved his grandchildren. When my daughter went back to work, her son wouldn't stay with a babysitter. John said that he would look after him, and they became really close. Our grandson came to dinner almost every night until he was eighteen. John loved his granddaughter, too, and there wasn't anything he wouldn't do for her. I remember the time when the family tried to put on a birthday party for him. John wanted nothing to do with it, and said he was too tired to attend. Our granddaughter phoned John from school and asked if he would drive her home. Of course, he couldn't refuse her, and that is how she managed to trick him into attending his birthday party. Years later, she named her baby son after John.

John and I cherished the memory of our fortieth anniversary. We had planned to go into Brandon to have dinner at a restaurant. The day before, I was babysitting my four-year-old grandson, Chris, and he said, "Grandma, you're not going into Brandon tomorrow. You're going down the street to the hall."

I immediately telephoned my daughter and asked her about my grandson's comment. She played the innocent and said that she knew nothing about it. When I continued to press her, she said, "Whom are you going to believe, a four-year-old or me?" I said that I was more inclined to believe the four-year-old, and I was right. Indeed, they had planned a big party for John and me at the Kinsman Hall. Friends

An aerial view of No. 33 SFTS at Carberry, Manitoba.
(Photo: Commonwealth Air Training Plan Museum)

from Brandon and Saskatchewan were in attendance, along with our relatives, including John's brother from England. John and I were overwhelmed as we walked into the hall that evening. I enjoyed watching my little grandson, who spilled the beans, dancing up a storm, and a great time was had by all. My mother said it was the best party she had ever attended. Our children knew that our wartime wedding had been very frugal, and they wanted to make it up to us. There was even a huge wedding cake. In later years, John and I often talked about the anniversary party that was almost a surprise.

We did go back to England to visit when we could afford it, but by the time we made our first visit, John's parents had died.

I'm eighty-three now, and I still enjoy my cottage at Clear Lake. I drive there by myself with my two dogs in my new car. I enjoy my cottage, but I do get a little lonely at times. Memories of happy times keep flooding back.

Rowena Hayball, December 2005

LESLIE (HOPPY) HOPTON

KELOWNA, BRITISH COLUMBIA

My husband never told anyone his real name because he always wanted to be called "Hoppy." He was born in Exmouth, England, and joined the RAF shortly after the war started. In December of 1940, he was sent to Canada as part of the groundcrew in airplane maintenance and was stationed at No. 33 SFTS in Carberry, Manitoba. The cold prairie winter was quite a shock to him, as it was to the other British airmen.

From time to time, dances were held at the station. Invitations were sent out to all the local girls in the area, and I received one too. I didn't go to many dances, but I did go to that one because it was on my birthday. Hoppy really wasn't a dancer, but he knew that was one way to meet the girls. I'm sure he must have had a couple of drinks before he got up enough courage to ask me to dance. That was the start of it, and we began to see each other when we could.

Hoppy became a regular guest at our farm at Wellwood for a year-and-a-half before we were married on June 18, 1942. We had the reception at the farm, and the Presbyterian minister came there to marry us. Most people in those days had their wedding receptions at their homes because they didn't have the money to do anything fancy. After the wedding, we boarded the train and spent our honeymoon in the big city of Winnipeg.

When we returned to Carberry, we rented a couple of rooms, but it wasn't really an apartment. It was just a bedsitter and a small kitchen. Actually, there wasn't a real kitchen either. We had only a hot plate and a few orange crates with little curtains where we stored our dishes. Although it was primitive by today's standards, we didn't think much about it because everybody seemed to be in the same boat. We were so much in love that we didn't notice our cold, dismal, and cramped surroundings.

An example of how primitive things were in those days can be exemplified by a funny incident that happened to another young couple in Carberry. In the apartment building where we lived, there was a common bathroom with no flush toilet. There was a metal bucket instead of a flush toilet, and we all took turns emptying it, although I can't remember where we put the contents. It certainly was not a pleasant task, and everyone usually put it off as long as possible. Anyway, one young husband tried to empty the bucket, but he discovered that it had frozen solid during one of Carberry's cold winter nights. In order to thaw it out, he put the bucket on the hot plate, and left the apartment for a while. When he returned, the contents of the bucket were merrily bubbling away on the hot plate. Word spread, and the young man took a lot of ribbing. I still laugh about that incident to this day.

Hoppy was sent back to Britain about Christmas 1943. There was a program that allowed wives of British servicemen to go to Britain during the war, but one had to agree to do war work. I agreed and couldn't wait to go. I signed the papers, and my friend, who had also married a British airman, and I took the train to New York and boarded the *Athlone Castle*. We were in the upper decks and the troops were down in the lower decks. It took ten days to cross in the convoy to Liverpool. We had to go to London to be equipped with gas masks, and then I proceeded to Wales, where Hoppy was stationed. I can't remember how to spell the name of the place because those Welsh words are really unusual. The Welsh people seem to use the letter "L" frequently in place names. We found a small apartment, and for my war work, I became a clerk at Hoppy's base. What luck! I later became pregnant, and our daughter was born in 1945.

After the war, Hoppy left the RAF, and we applied to come to Canada, but there

Carberry, Manitoba, in wartime.
(Photo: Carberry Plains Archives)

Snow removal at No. 33 SFTS was a thankless, but necessary task.
(Photo: Commonwealth Air Training Plan Museum)

was no room on any of the ships. He had always enjoyed his time in Canada, and he knew this was where he wanted to spend the rest of his life. We waited, and in the meantime, Hoppy got a job as a conductor on a bus. Finally, we got fed up and booked passage on a plane, and we arrived back at the farm in Wellwood, Manitoba, in the winter of 1947. Hoppy joined the RCAF after he arrived in Canada, and we lived at various places across the country. I have fond memories of Rivers, Camp Borden, Goose Bay, Trenton, and Ottawa.

Hoppy left the RCAF when all three branches of the military were amalgamated [in 1968]. He took a Dale Carnegie course and got a job in Ottawa giving talks and conducting tours in a museum. This was his calling, and he especially loved conducting school tours.

We had always wanted to go to British Columbia, but we decided to wait until our children were older. In 1967, we went to Kelowna to visit friends, and were told that a nearby lot was coming up for sale. We put in a bid, and continued on to Vancouver Island to finish our holiday. When we returned to Kelowna, we discovered that our bid had been accepted. We decided that we didn't want a mortgage, so we returned to Ottawa where we both worked for the government for the next five years in order to save money to build our dream house on that lot in Kelowna.

On October 19, 1972, we left Ottawa in our trailer, but it took us six months to get to Kelowna. We took our time, travelling down the East Coast to Mexico and to other interesting places. On April 20, 1973, we arrived in Kelowna and started to build our home.

There are now three children, eight grandchildren and five great-grandchildren. Sadly, Hoppy has passed away, and I now live in a seniors' residence in Kelowna. My sister, Kathleen Harris Maguire,[8] also had a war groom husband, but he has passed away, too.

Hazel Hopton, November 2005

---

[8] See Ken Harris's story.

TOM HUNTER

CHARLOTTETOWN, PRINCE EDWARD ISLAND

I was born in Kilmarnock, Ayrshire, Scotland. I joined the RAF and was posted overseas to Charlottetown, Prince Edward Island, in March of 1940. After arriving in Halifax, I was sent to No. 31 General Reconnaissance School just outside of Charlottetown, where I was part of the groundcrew that serviced the planes on the station.

Naturally, we airmen always gravitated to town on our leaves. One day while in Charlottetown, I was walking in Victoria Park with three of my friends when I saw my future wife, Eileen, and two of her friends near the old cannons by the waterfront. Everyone started chatting, and because Eileen and I were the shy ones, the others actually introduced us to each other. I am six-foot-one-and-a-half-inches, and I looked down at this five-foot-nothing, young lady. I knew I had to see her again. I guess she liked my Scottish accent, so she agreed to see me. We did the usual things that young couples did at that time. We attended dances, enjoyed long walks, and went to the movies. We even attended church together. Because Eileen loved to skate, she took me to the arena and proceeded to teach me, although I had never been on

Tom and Eileen Hunter on their sixtieth anniversary. (Photo: Hunter Family)

Tom and Eileen Hunter shortly after they were married.
(Photo: Hunter Family)

skates before. Eventually, I developed into a pretty good skater, if I do say so myself.

I'll never forget how well the Canadians treated us airmen. All of us were welcomed by the local families, and I was lucky to be adopted by a farm family just outside of town. They always made sure that we had lots to eat, and we young fellows always seemed to be hungry. On my time off, when I wasn't with Eileen, I was at the farm, and she always knew where to find me

Because Eileen's parents lived outside of town, she and her sister shared an apartment in Charlottetown. I didn't know it at the time, but Eileen had another boyfriend who worked on the railroad, and he came to see her on weekends. For a while, she juggled both of us, seeing me during the week and him on weekends, but eventually she dumped the other fellow.

After we became serious, Eileen brought me home to meet her parents. They were a little hesitant at first because they thought I might have a wife back in Scotland, but they came around and accepted me as a future son-in-law. I proposed one evening when we were at Eileen's apartment after two years of courtship, and we were married in June 1943 in St. Dunstan's Basilica.

I have it on authority that fifty-two RAF fellows married Island girls but, to my knowledge, there are only four of us left on the Island. Some of the couples went back to the U.K. to live, some of the marriages didn't last, and others have passed away. In fact, one of the airmen from my group of friends in Victoria Park married one of Eileen's friends.

I was posted to the U.K. in March of 1944. Our daughter was born in September 1944. I didn't want Eileen and the baby to come to Britain during the war because I had no idea where I would be sent, and it wouldn't be fair to leave them in a strange country living with my parents in Scotland. I was posted to various bases in the U.K., and when the end to the European War was in sight, I was transferred to the Highland Light Infantry in the spring of 1945. The war with Japan was expected to go on for some time, and ground troops were needed in the Far East. Then, the war ended unexpectedly after the atomic bombs were dropped, and I was sent to Greece as part of the Occupational Forces. I returned to the U.K. in August of 1946 and was demobilized. I told the authorities that my home was in Canada, and they arranged passage for me.

By the time I arrived in Charlottetown, most of the good jobs had been taken by returning Canadian servicemen, but I managed to get a job in an American canning company. Later, I was employed by the federal government as the foreman at the Research Station on the Island. I worked there for thirty years and have long since retired.

Eileen and I have seven children—five girls and two boys. To date, we have seven grandchildren and one great-grandson. We still live in the home we built in 1948. I have absolutely no regrets about moving to Canada, although we have been back to Scotland several times to see my brothers and their families, and we have enjoyed our visits.

If we live till June, we will have been married for sixty-three years. We had a big celebration for our sixtieth wedding anniversary, and it is a day that Eileen and I will never forget. Our son is in the Canadian Forces and is part of a re-enactment group in Gagetown, New Brunswick. For parades and other events, members of the group dress up in World War II uniforms and drive the old vehicles from that time. On our sixtieth wedding anniversary, we walked out of the house to get into the car, and when we opened the garage door, we saw this old army jeep decorated with streamers, pom-poms, and a sign saying "Just Married 60 Years." Everyone insisted that this was to be our vehicle for the day, and we reluctantly climbed in. We were driven to Victoria Park where we had met sixty years before, and we posed for photographs. We were then driven all over Charlottetown, and everyone we saw waved and cheered. Eileen and I laugh about it now, but we were a little embarrassed by all the attention lavished upon us. The event was even written up in a seniors' magazine.

Life has been good to us, and we are still very much in love. Eileen calls me her "war bride," but I tell her that I'm really her "POW."

May 2006

JOHN INGLIS

ST. CATHARINES, ONTARIO

My father, John Inglis, is currently living in a seniors' residence in Carleton Place, Ontario. After the death of my mother and a busy life in Canada, his memories of the past are now a bit hazy. However, with the help of my family, my parents' friends, photos, and memorabilia, I think I can piece together his story with a fair degree of accuracy.

Dad was born in 1921 in Motherwell, Scotland, a steel town about twelve miles outside of Glasgow. He lived on a street called Windmill Hill Way. The name sounded so lovely and picturesque to me when I was a child. I found out later, however, that Motherwell was basically a gritty, gray, and rather depressed working-class town.

John and Jean Inglis on their wedding day.
(Photo: Inglis Family)

Dad left school at the age of fourteen and went to work as a moulder in a steel mill. Although money was limited, his family was always generous and hospitable to visitors and strangers, a tradition that Dad continued throughout his life. Despite a lack of formal education, Dad, like his father before him, loved books and was well read. He could quote Robbie Burns, Robert Service, and the Rubaiyat of Omar Khayyam by heart, particularly after "a wee dram or two."

Despite the objections of his mother, Dad enlisted in the RAF as soon as he turned eighteen. His two older brothers had already joined the army, and my grandmother was extremely reluctant to see her last and youngest enlist. Fortunately, all three of her boys survived.

Dad was selected for pilot training and was sent to No. 9 Elementary Service Flying Training School in St. Catharines, Ontario, in 1942. He had done well flying the Tiger Moths in England, but he was not as successful in Canada, mainly because of his cavalier attitude. The pilot trainees were required to practise precautionary landings as part of their training. They were to pick a spot and then fly down to about twelve to fifteen feet above it before increasing their altitude in order to complete another circuit. Dad and an equally cocky friend had taken to actually bouncing briefly on the tarmac before taking off again. Unfortunately, an instructor followed them one day and caught them. Thus, their training as a pilots came to an abrupt end. When he was relating this story to me, Dad said, "You were supposed to do what you were told, you know." Obviously, doing exactly what he was told did not come naturally for Dad who has always had a bit of a cheeky streak in him.

Although Dad's pilot training in St. Catharines was not successful, his love life definitely was. While he was in St. Catharines, a group of trainees decided to take a boat cruise on Lake Ontario. While on the boat, Dad noticed another airman talking to a very attractive young woman with thick auburn hair. Dad evidently decided that he should be the one doing the chatting, and he joined the conversation. The whirlwind romance that developed during that summer lasted for almost sixty years.

My mother, Jean Bouskill, was a sixteen-year-old Toronto high school student who was spending her summer at a farmerette camp. Because of the "farmerette" initiative, more than 900 young women were recruited as agricultural workers and were placed in the Niagara fruit belt of Ontario. At that time, a labour shortage in agriculture had developed because many young men had enlisted. My grandmother was not keen on the idea that her daughter was going to live in an unsupervised camp and voiced her objections. My mother was, however, headstrong and possessed considerable powers of persuasion. She talked my grandmother into allowing her to go, "to support the war effort." The "guilt trip" strategy worked. Needless to say, my grandmother was fit to be tied when her sixteen-year-old daughter returned home at the end of the summer and announced that she was engaged to a Scottish airman. My grandmother told Mom in no uncertain terms to end the engagement and to go back to school to finish her education.

While my grandmother thought that Mom was far too young to be engaged, my mother's family did welcome my Dad's visits. My mother was the second eldest of six children, and as a result, Dad, not only had to win her heart, but he also had to ingratiate himself to her sisters and her brother. The dashing young airman obviously made quite an impression because Aunt Eleanor, Mom's sister, can still recite his name, rank and serial number. My aunt remembers Dad taking her to the store for ice cream. Dad wanted to spend time alone with my mother, and the treats for her younger sisters were a bribe in order to accomplish his goal. Uncle Larry, Mom's brother, however, proved to be even more challenging. During one visit to my grandmother's house, Dad discovered my uncle putting fancy holes in his air force dress shirt with a hole punch. On another occasion, while Dad and Mom were walking back from an outing, my uncle surprised them, pretending to be a burglar. He even had a stocking over his head.

After Dad washed out of pilot training, he was offered a number of options. Still wanting to fly, he chose to go to gunnery school in Mont Joli, Quebec. He evidently followed instructions more carefully that time, and he successfully graduated as an air gunner. At Mont Joli, his multi-national crew was assembled. The crew of his B25 Mitchell Bomber was made up of a Canadian pilot, an Aussie wireless operator / air gunner, an English navigator, and a Scottish mid-upper-gunner—my dad. My parents were parted when Dad was posted to the U.K.

Dad never spoke much about the time he was on operations with No. 139 Wing, which was stationed in England and Belgium. It was certainly an unsettling period in his life, to say the least. He and his crew completed their tour of thirty-five trips over Germany and occupied territory and were awarded the 1939–45 France and German Star. I do remember looking at photos of his squadron and asking Dad about his friends. I was shocked to learn that many of them did not survive the war.

Throughout the time when Dad was on active service, his young fiancée from Toronto was never far from his thoughts. Dad tried to write daily letters and lovingly signed them, "Your wee boy."

After graduating from high school, Mom got a secretarial job with a Toronto company. All was not well on the home front, however. My mother was having second thoughts abut her engagement to the Scottish airman so far away. Mom loved to dance and have fun, and there were numerous young men about who were happy to oblige. Sitting at home and waiting for her fiancé to return from the war evidently did not hold much appeal for her, and she didn't take well to having her wings clipped. Consequently, she broke off the engagement and mailed Dad's ring back to him. Dad's "Dear John" letter left him heartbroken, but he was persistent, and he continued to write to her faithfully, even after the engagement was off.

After the war ended, Dad was demobilized and returned to his home in Motherwell. There were few employment prospects for him or anyone else in Scotland at that time. Therefore, Dad decided to take the plunge, and he arranged to emigrate to

Canada. While his mother had reservations about this venture, his own father had actually visited Canada in his youth, and he encouraged Dad to go.

Conversely, my mother in Toronto was not enthusiastic when she learned that Dad was planning to emigrate because she was not sure if she wanted to pursue the relationship, and she told him so. Dad said he was coming anyway and wrote, "If only to visit your family." Dad arrived in Halifax on the *Aquitania* on May 25, 1947, and then boarded a train to Toronto. His persistence paid off! My mother told me that she flew into his arms the moment he stepped off the train at Union Station. A short time later, after taking a week off work to spend some time with him, she told her best friend, "It's as if John has never been away." The magic of the summer of 1942 was rekindled after a separation of almost five years. To the tune of "Always," and wearing a gown made by her mother, Mom married Dad in my grandmother's house on May 21, 1948, almost a year after Dad arrived in Canada.

Everyone pulled together to help Mom and Dad get established. Initially, the newlyweds lived at my grandmother's home. My mother's boss at the Industrial Accident Prevention Association used his connections to help Dad find a job, and he was hired by International Harvester in Hamilton. Dad began work as a moulder, the same type of work he did in Scotland before the war, and he eventually worked his way up to a managerial position. He stayed with the same company until his retirement.

At first, my mother remained at my grandmother's house while Dad boarded in Hamilton during the week. He returned to Toronto and his bride on weekends. When a clerical position in the office of International Harvester opened up in Hamilton, Mom applied and was hired. At last, my parents were able to begin their lives together. They rented an apartment and, later, bought a house and began to raise a family.

After Dad came to Canada, he left the past behind him and rarely looked back. He told me that one of the first things he did after arriving in Canada was to give away his tweed jacket and brogues, and he tried to adopt a Canadian accent. Whenever he was asked if he was Scottish, he would often say, "No, I'm a Canadian, and I have the papers to prove it. Do you?" One of the few tributes to his Scottish roots was our childhood pet, a border collie named Hamish.

My father returned to Scotland only once, and that was only because my grandfather died. After looking up one of his best friends, Dad was distressed to discover that this man had become a wasted alcoholic. I think that discovery made him realize more than ever that his move to Canada had been most fortunate.

Dad and Mom spent most of their married lives in the Hamilton area, and my brother and I were both born there. Because of his own experiences, Dad always had a soft spot in his heart for recent immigrants and was always ready to lend a hand to anyone he met who had recently arrived in Canada. As a result, we got to meet many new and interesting people from many parts of the world. Upon retirement, my parents moved to the village of Marmora, Ontario, as Dad had always liked the idea of living in a small town. Dad ran for town council and also served as deputy reeve for the village. My parents had two children and five grandchildren.

My parents maintained strong links to the friends they made when they first married, and they made many new friends along the way. My mother became ill in 2002 and died. My father was devastated. Shortly after her death, Dad told me that he had made a point of telling my mother that he loved her every day of their married lives. Clearly, Dad has never regretted his decision to "horn in" on the conversation between the pretty auburn-haired sixteen-year-old girl and the unknown airman over sixty years ago.

Judy Inglis, December 2006

GORDON CHARLES KEATCH

WINNIPEG, MANITOBA

I was born in Melbourne, Australia, on April 30, 1924. A job at the post office delivering telegrams exposed me to the rhythm of Morse code. When I was seventeen, I joined the air cadets, and I found this experience to be interesting and educational.

On my eighteenth birthday, I tried to enlist in RAAF, but aircrews were not being recruited at the time because there was a greater need for army personnel. The Pacific War had started, and Australia was in grave danger of attack from the Japanese. I decided to join the Australian Artillery, as my brother was by then a captain in that section. I became a gun-layer, aiming and elevating the gun, and spent the next twenty months at several locations about the country. By 1943, there was an increased demand for aircrews in Europe. Almost anyone who wanted to re-muster into the RAAF was allowed to transfer, and that's what I did.

Having a great desire to be sent to Canada for air training, I decided to use the system to my advantage. Since most recruits wanted to be pilots, I decided to apply as a wireless/air gunner. Also, preference was given to older personnel for overseas postings, and by then I was approaching the mature age of twenty! By December 1943, I was at Initial Training School, and six weeks later, I was on an old World War I American vessel, along with many wounded American soldiers, bound for San Francisco.

From San Francisco, we travelled by train to Vancouver and continued on to Brandon for a few days before stopping at Winnipeg. I was posted to No. 3 Wireless

School on Shafestbury Boulevard, the former School for the Deaf. We lived in the newly constructed huts on the grounds and took our meals and courses in the main building. My exposure to Morse code at the post office in Australia came into play, and I was able to learn it reasonably quickly. We also had to learn aircraft recognition and wireless theory. The course lasted

Gordon and Anne Keatch on their wedding day.
(Photo: Keatch Family)

about six months, and we were given a mid-term leave, a week in Minneapolis for me. Our weekends were usually free. Towards the end of the course, we did air-to-ground training flights from the Winnipeg airport.

The most exciting part of the war for me was the time spent in Winnipeg because I met my wife there. On our free time, many of the airmen from the Wireless School would head to downtown Winnipeg. Two service clubs were always open to us, the United Services Club in Eaton's Annex and the Airmen's Club on Donald Street. At these places, we could get a cheap meal, but, more importantly, we got a chance to dance with many of the local girls. Anne Rowley was a hostess at the Airmen's Club, and we started to see each other whenever we could. I was welcomed by her parents and enjoyed many wonderful meals at her home. Since Anne and I both loved to dance, we attended many of them around Winnipeg. We enjoyed going to the Winnipeg Auditorium [now the Provincial Archives Building] on Saturday nights to watch sporting events, such as basketball games or boxing matches. I remember seeing Joe Louis there when he came to referee the fights. Dances usually followed these sporting events at the Winnipeg Auditorium, much to our delight.

Now that we had the wireless training, it was time to do some practical work on the guns. I was sent to No. 5 Bombing and Gunnery School in Dafoe, Saskatchewan. It was a six-week course, and we finished just before Christmas 1944. I was one of the fortunate ones to receive a commission. Back in Winnipeg, my final leave was spent on a trip to New York via Toronto. It was a most interesting experience, and I was impressed with the warm welcome I received from the Americans. Upon returning to Winnipeg, I learned that I was to be sent back to Australia because the war in Europe was winding down. Events were still rather hectic in the Pacific Theatre, however, and there was a need for aircrew there.

Before returning to Australia, we were posted to Calgary for a month. There, I learned all about chinooks, a word not in my vocabulary at the time. A friend and I had gone into Calgary one day for some five-pin bowling, and because it was a lovely February afternoon, we were not wearing overcoats. On the way back, the temperature suddenly plummeted. We had taken the streetcar to the end of the line and started on the long walk to the base. Needless to say, we were freezing! An American in a jeep picked us up, but we were even colder in that open vehicle because of the increased wind chill. As a result of our experience, my friend and I ended up with frostbite. We learned about the deceptive nature of a chinook the hard way.

It was then on to San Francisco by train where we spent two weeks waiting for a ship to take us to Australia. On the return journey, our ship stopped at Guadalcanal to drop off supplies. The devastation from the six-month battle between the Americans and the Japanese was very much in evidence. Sunken ships and other equipment littered the port, and the vegetation was just beginning to recover. By the time I returned home to Australia, I had been away for more than a year.

Following a short leave, I reported to a conversion course in Ballarat, Victoria. We had been trained on British radio equipment in Canada, but now we were to be flying in Liberators which were equipped with American radios. Shortly after starting the program, the atomic bombs were dropped on Japan, and the war was over. I was duty officer in Ballarat the day the war with Japan ended. VJ Day was a memorable experience. By September 1945, I was demobilized.

When the time came for me to leave Winnipeg back in January 1945, Anne and I said our good-byes, but we continued to correspond. Once out of the Service, I asked Anne to come to Australia to marry me. Anne agreed, but she didn't come alone, however. As the train continued on its westward journey, it picked up several Canadian war brides destined for Australia, including Doris Fairman from Calgary. She befriended Anne and became a bridesmaid at our wedding.

Anne's parents were devastated, of course, as they thought they would never see their daughter again. My family, on the other hand, was ecstatic, and they were delighted and charmed by this Canadian girl who came all the way to Australia to marry me.

On November 23, 1946, Anne and I were married in Melbourne. About twenty people were in attendance, and my brother was best man.

Anne got a job at the Department of Aircraft Production and we enjoyed a busy social life as newlyweds, still dancing, of course. In time, my wife missed her family, and we decided to return to Canada. I didn't need much persuasion since I had enjoyed my time in Canada and, in retrospect, it was the best decision I ever made, apart from marrying Anne. It was now my mother's turn to be the disappointed parent.

My now pregnant wife and I arrived back in Winnipeg in November 1948. Our first son, Ron, was born in April 1949, and our second son, Donald, was born in 1950. After some short-term work, I started a cost accounting course which took about five years. Meanwhile, I found employment at Kipp Kelly Limited, a machinery-manufacturing firm where I stayed for thirty-three years. I retired in 1983 as the vice-president and general manager.

While living in Winnipeg, I became involved in several local organizations. I was president of Silver Heights Community Club, school trustee and chairman with the St. James School Board, alderman for the St. James City Council, and president of the Niakwa Country Club. Other interests included the Manitoba Theatre Centre and the Down Under Club for Australian and New Zealand ex-air force members who had also moved to Winnipeg.

There has always been the lingering question of "what if?" Supposing the RAAF accepted me in 1942 when I first applied? Would I have come to Canada? Would I have met Anne? Not likely! Fate takes some strange twists in one's life and, as it turned out, it was very good to me. I met a girl who became a wonderful wife and a devoted mother. We have enjoyed a great life and have travelled all over the Pacific and Europe. Our wonderful family now includes three grandchildren and one great-grandson. We look forward to celebrating our sixtieth wedding anniversary in November 2006.

September 2006

BOB KELLOW

WINNIPEG, MANITOBA

Bob and Doreen Kellow are both deceased, but I was able to talk to their daughter, Jan Connon, about her parents' love story and Bob's personal life. Before he died, Bob wrote a detailed account of his experiences with No. 617 Squadron and with the underground movement. Paths to Freedom *was published after Bob's death, and his book is the source of this story.*

Bob was born in New Castle, Australia. After he enlisted in the RAAF, he was posted to Canada in 1941 to train as a wireless operator at No. 3 Wireless School in Winnipeg. Emily and John Smith opened their home to the young airmen from overseas, and Bob became one of their regular visitors. When their daughter, Doreen, and Bob met, it was another classic case of "love at first sight." Doreen had just graduated from nurses' training and was working with the St. John's Ambulance Corps.

Jan related an amusing incident that occurred during her parents' courtship. Bob wanted to help the family and offered to clear away the snow after one of Winnipeg's famous blizzards. To everyone's astonishment, Bob cleared not only the sidewalk, but also the front lawn. It wasn't long before Bob learned how to deal with Winnipeg winters in a more efficient manner.

Doreen had had one serious relationship before she met Bob, but Jan didn't know if Bob did. Like many other young couples at the time, they went to dances and enjoyed going to Grand Beach by train. Bob proposed at a dance, and they became engaged before he was posted to England to serve with Bomber Command. They corresponded regularly when Bob was overseas, and their daughter still has all their letters.

Bob completed a tour of operations with No. 50 RAF Squadron. A new squadron, No. 617, had just been formed, and Bob was selected, along with many other airmen who had distinguished themselves during their tours of operations. This new squadron was assigned difficult and dangerous tasks, and intense training was required.

The squadron's first task was to rupture the Moehne and Eder Dams in Germany's Rühr Valley with a new type of bomb. This action was intended to damage the

*Bob and Doreen Kellow shortly after
Doreen arrived in Australia.*
(Photo: Janice Connon)

power plants in the area, thereby reducing Germany's industrial capacity. After successfully breaching the dams, No. 617 received a great deal of publicity and became known thereafter as the Dam Busters.[9]

No. 617 had other operations of a similar nature. In September 1943, while Bob and the crew were returning from a raid on the Dortmund–Ems Canal in Germany, their Lancaster, affectionately called Nan, became disabled after hitting some trees in the fog near the drop area. The crew managed to drop their 12,000-pound bomb, but the plane was severely crippled and had to be abandoned. While the pilot, Les Knight, held the plane steady, the crew parachuted out over occupied Holland. The crew landed safely, except for Les, who was killed when the plane crashed. The crew of the doomed Lancaster owed their lives to Les Knight's courage. When Doreen learned that Bob was missing in occupied territory, she was devastated.

Bob was determined to avoid capture at all costs. Fortunately, many people from the underground movement in Holland, Belgium and France were willing to risk their lives to help Bob elude the Germans. To make a long story short, he was passed along through the underground, and was able to reach Spain, a neutral country. From there, he was sent to Gibraltar, and then, back to England. Although the story sounds so simple and easy, the journey was long, tedious, dangerous, and exhausting. Bob was always mindful of the risk that his benefactors were taking on his behalf, and he was always on edge.

Throughout all the time Bob was on the run in occupied territory, he was comforted by a little hobnailed boot that he carried with him during operations. In the little boot, Bob kept a small white elephant that Doreen had given him for good luck, a leaf from the park where they had walked, the cork from the first bottle of

---

[9] Paul Brickhill wrote a book about this action called *The Dam Busters* (1951); there is also an Oscar-nominated movie of the same name (1954).

wine that they had shared, and a copy of a prayer. The little boot is now one of their daughter's prized possessions.

After Bob returned to England, he visited No. 617 Squadron and was shocked to learn that their numbers were severely depleted. So many fine young men had been killed or captured during operations. He was told that the rear gunner and the flight engineer from his crew were prisoners of war, but he was thankful that they were alive. Bob was delighted to learn that the other members of his crew were passed along through the underground as he had been, and had their own adventures before reaching freedom. The news of Les Knight's death, however, was a devastating blow for Bob. The two friends had promised each other that if anything happened to either one of them, the survivor would visit the parents of the deceased. Bob kept his promise, as difficult as it was, and paid his respects to Les's parents in Australia.

After Bob returned to England after successfully eluding the Germans, he was given a choice of postings. Since he felt that no pilot could ever replace Les, he chose not to return to No. 617 Squadron and, instead, requested a posting to Australia. There, he served with Transport Command until he was demobilized in 1946.

After his demobilization, Bob sent word to Doreen, and she was able to arrange passage to Australia. Doreen's family was sad to see her go, of course, but they realized that she was determined to be with Bob. They knew their daughter was marrying a fine man. Bob's parents were delighted with Doreen, and she completely captivated the entire family.

Bob and Doreen were married in Australia and resumed their lives. When they returned to Canada to visit Doreen's family, Bob investigated the job market in Winnipeg and was hired by Manitoba Hydro. He worked there for twenty-nine years, starting out as a draftsman and retiring as an executive assistant in 1982.

In later years, Bob returned to Europe to retrace his journey with the underground movement and was able to make contact with some of the people who had helped him reach safety. In Holland, he became an honorary mayor in the village where he landed after jumping from the plane. Bob had buried his parachute upon landing, but a local farmer had dug it up and burned it to prevent the Germans from finding it. He did, however, keep the handle, and he gave it to Bob many years later.

Bob always enjoyed air force reunions and attended several in Australia, Canada and the U.K. Jan remembers accompanying her father in 1976 to one reunion in Scampton where the Dam Busters were stationed and was treated like royalty.

Jan said that her father would often "clam up" when talking about the war, and the sight of blood and scenes of violence on television really bothered him. On their first operation, Bob and his crew returned to the drop area to see if their bomb had successfully breached the dam. Bob told his daughter that it was the most horrific experience to see the massive devastation that resulted from their bombing action, and he said he was badly shaken. He received the Distinguished Flying Medal for that operation, and although that award was his most prestigious medal, he chose not to wear it on parade.

Bob became a citizen shortly after he came to Canada, and he had no regrets about leaving Australia. Winnipeg was his home, and he became a valued member of the community. He joined several organizations, such as the Royal Air Force Escaping Society, the RCAF Auxiliary (Reserve), and the Down Under Club, to name a few. He was past president of the Wartime Pilots' and Observers' Association.

Bob died on February 12, 1988, at the young age of seventy-one. Bob and Doreen had two children, a son and a daughter.

June 2005

LIONEL LEVENSON

WINNIPEG, MANITOBA

My husband, Lionel Levenson, was born in London, England, on September 9, 1921, and joined the RAF in 1941. He took his initial training in England and was sent to Carberry, Manitoba, in 1942 for advanced flight training. While on leave in Winnipeg, Lionel attended a social. There, he met my girlfriend, and he said to her, "Are there any more at home like you?" It certainly wasn't the most original line in the world. Anyway, she mentioned that her best friend was at home, and Lionel asked to meet her. The "her" happened to be "me." He obtained my phone number and called me about 9 p.m. that evening. It was New Year's Day, 1943, and he asked if he could come over right away. I replied that it was far too late, but he was insistent. I agreed very reluctantly, and the rest is history. It was a fast, whirlwind courtship. That's the way it was in wartime.

We started to see each other as often as we could, and Lionel would stay at my home in Winnipeg whenever he was on leave. We both knew almost from the time we met that we were serious. Lionel didn't propose as such because we both just knew that marriage was inevitable. I remember going to the wings parade in Carberry when Lionel graduated.

Just two months after meeting, we became engaged on March 3, 1943, and two months later, we were married on May 5. At the time of our marriage, I was all of eighteen, and Lionel was twenty-one. My mother died when I was eight and my grandmother had raised my sister and me. My father, to his credit, never raised any objections to the marriage. He asked me only one question, "Are you sure?" Even when he learned that I would be crossing through U-boat-infested waters to England, he never said a word. My father really liked Lionel and came to regard him as the son he never had. Conversely, Lionel's mother back in England was really upset about the marriage. She thought that her son had fallen into the hands of a wicked woman, and I think she always felt that I stole her son away from her.

By wartime standards, the guest list for our wedding was huge. My father wasn't going to skimp on anything for his oldest daughter's wedding. My gown was designed by the first dress designer Winnipeg ever had. The wedding, with more than 200 guests, was held at Picardy's on Broadway. My grandmother was always working for and giving to the community, and so she had to invite everybody. My sister was my maid of honour, and Lionel asked somebody from his base to be his best man. We spent our honeymoon at the old Fort Garry Hotel and had a beautiful suite. Although it was May, it turned cold and snowed heavily the next day. After all, this was Winnipeg! I had to ask my father to bring my winter coat to the hotel.

When I met Lionel, he was in the final stages of his pilot training. He was very bright and was always at the top of his classes. In fact, he later became a member of the Mensa Club for those in the top one per cent in intelligence. He was chosen to become a pilot instructor and was posted to Vulcan, Alberta. After that, he had postings in North Battleford, Saskatchewan, and Red Deer, Alberta, and I, of course, went with him to these and other places.

I especially remember one occurrence during Lionel's training days before our marriage. He was coming in for a landing at night at Carberry. The night was as black as could be, and although he could not see well on his landing approach to the runway, he landed safely and went to bed. To his surprise, the next morning, he was woken early and told to report immediately to the commanding officer, who questioned him on what had happened to his aircraft. In the morning daylight, Lionel was shocked to see that both the wingtips had been sheared off to within inches of cutting critical control wires that would have led to a fatal crash. Following investigation, it was found that his wings had been clipped by low-lying telephone cables suspended between poles at the start of the runway approach. His commanding officer told him that he wouldn't be penalized, and said that anybody who could pull himself out of that situation was too good a pilot to be charged.

Despite this accident, in fact,

Lionel and Beatrice Levenson
on their wedding day.
(Photo: Levenson Family)

Lionel was rated as above the average pilot.

Lionel was an instructor for almost three years before he received the news that he was to be sent back to England. I wanted to go, too, and I actually travelled across the Atlantic two weeks before Lionel did. I went in a convoy in January 1945, and it was fifteen days of constant seasickness. I, however, didn't let seasickness get me down, as I wanted to see and experience everything. If we went out on deck, we had to hold onto ropes. There was an aircraft carrier next to us in the convoy. From it, single-engine planes would take off, search for U-boats, and then land. The pilots, who were hardly more that kids, used to wave to us. It was such dangerous work because the swells were between fifteen and thirty feet high. I don't know how they did it with the carrier bobbing up and down.

Two of the ships in the convoy carried a few war brides, as well as war materiel. I think there were about a dozen ships in the convoy, and it was very, very rough. As I recall, we lost some tanks and lifeboats that were lashed to the deck because of the conditions. Because of U-boat activity, depth charges were dropped over the side, and the whole ship would shake.

Three or four of us were officers' wives, and the rest were servicemen's wives. The wives of officers were treated differently, I can tell you. We sat with the captain of the ship at mealtimes, and the other wives were regarded as the "common people." The British class system was in evidence, and I couldn't get over it. It all seemed so silly to me because we were all the same.

We landed in Liverpool and, from there, I boarded the train to my destination. My husband had told me to get off the train at each station to ensure that I could see where my luggage was going, and I did just that. One time, the train stopped in the middle of nowhere, and I didn't get off because there wasn't a station to be seen. Wouldn't you know it? That's when my luggage disappeared. Eventually, I did meet up with my luggage, but it was a stressful time.

I was going to Frome, Somerset, where my in-laws were staying. They met me at the station, but they only knew me from a photograph. I got off the train, and my mother-in-law stared at my beaver coat, an unusual sight in England. Frome was a very old, quaint village, just like out of a fairy tale. My in-laws had left London because of the bombing and went to Bath, where the bombing was just as bad. They moved again, this time to Frome. My mother-in-law had bought a piece of property on the main so that she could open a men's wear shop. A pretty little stream went down the middle of the street. We lived in an old, old house, in which the floor of the bedroom where I slept tilted steeply. My husband's twin sisters, the housekeeper, and I all shared that bedroom.

For all intents and purposes, my mother-in-law and I got along, but it took a real effort on my part. She was a businesswoman and was used to having her own way about everything. I was different. I was willing to compromise.

The rationing was severe. I had my own little ration book. I could have one egg a week, a couple of little pats of butter, and a tiny bit of meat. My mother-in-law kept chickens under the house, and we enjoyed those from time to time.

My husband arrived two weeks later, and I followed him around to all the places where he was posted. Lionel would go ahead and find lodging for me in farm homes near his bases. I enjoyed making hot chocolate for Lionel and his friends. I used to go to the fence that surrounded the base and pass the hot chocolate through to them.

Lionel was in a Mosquito squadron and, ironically, his navigator was afraid of flying. He was such an interesting fellow and had chosen to become a navigator because of the long period of training. He thought that, with any luck, the war would be over by the time he finished his course. The squadron flew at night to occupied territory, but I never worried about Lionel much because he was such a good pilot.

I loved my time in England. To me, it was all one big adventure. I remember when Lionel and I were in London at the time of the V2 rockets. We were on the top level of a double-decker bus with a group of schoolgirls when a V2 was sighted. All of a sudden, the bus shook violently from the explosion. The schoolgirls laughed and shouted, "It missed us!"

When Lionel was posted to Red Deer, Alberta, I made friends with a girl who had also married an RAF fellow. Later, in England, I discovered that she lived near me, and we supported each other.

As the war was winding down, Lionel received the news that he was to be posted overseas again, this time to India. During the six months that he was in India, he rose to become commanding officer of No. 84 Mosquito Squadron, but then the war ended. On the ship to India, Lionel played bridge with other servicemen, and because he had a photographic memory, he knew exactly what cards each of the players was holding. He won so much money that he didn't have to use his wages while he was in India.

At the end of his tour, Lionel returned to Britain and was discharged in the spring of 1946. I didn't have to talk my husband into coming to Canada. When he saw how things were going with his mother and me, he said, "We'll go home." Lionel's family was quite wealthy, and he could have lived a prosperous life in England, but he wasn't interested.

Air flights to North America had just resumed, and we were able to fly to New

One of the many buildings at No. 33 SFTS.
(Photo: Commonwealth Air Training Plan Museum)

York and then to Chicago. We took the train from Chicago to Winnipeg.

My father was ecstatic when he learned that we were coming back to Canada. He told Lionel that whatever business venture he was in, Lionel would be part of it. My father and his partners bought the Norwood Hotel, and Lionel was the manager for a few years. Lionel wasn't crazy about the hotel business, especially the "beer parlour" part of it. After a few years, the fellow who sold the hotel to them wanted to buy the hotel back, and they agreed. My father and Lionel continued to have more successful business ventures.

Our son was born in April 1950.

Lionel had absolutely no regrets about leaving England. He loved Canada and Winnipeg. He became a Canadian citizen as soon as he could, but I can't remember the date. We did return to England to visit quite often, and we got along with most of the relatives very, very well.

Former RAF aircrew formed a club in Winnipeg some years ago, and asked Lionel to join. He declined and said, "I came to Canada, and from now on, I'm a Canadian."

Sadly, after sixty years together, my loving husband died peacefully of natural causes at the age of eighty-one in August 2003.

Beatrice Levenson, July 2006

JAMES ROBERT (BOB) COWAN MACBAIN

CASTLEGAR, BRITISH COLUMBIA

I was born in Edinburgh, Scotland, on October 2, 1919. In 1938 I joined the RAF and was sent to Canada in 1942 to be part of the BCATP. I was posted to No. 34 Service Flying Training School in Medicine Hat, Alberta.

The airmen from No. 34 often spent their leaves in Nelson, British Columbia. The people there welcomed us with open arms, and we were able to stay at the homes of the local families. There was no shortage of invitations to the many functions in the area.

I met Marjorie Jorgensen at a party in Nelson in 1944, but I can't remember who hosted the party. After Marjorie and I were introduced, I mentioned that I was going to a beach party the next day, and she said she was going, too. What luck! That was the start of it.

We courted for about six months and were married in December 1945. Although Marjorie's mother favoured the marriage, her father didn't. Just before we were married, he asked Marjorie if she still intended to marry that "so-and-so" Englishman, but he used a stronger adjective to describe me. She replied that she certainly did intend to marry me.

My family back home was very happy about the marriage, but they didn't meet Marjorie until 1949 when we took a trip back to the U.K. By then, my father had died and my mother had remarried. My new stepfather was very supportive, and my sister, who was a nurse in the RAF during the war, was especially delighted to meet Marjorie.

During the time I was posted at No. 34 SFTS, I went with a group of airmen to tour an electric power plant in the area. The president of West Kootenay Power and Light Company, our tour conductor, said that if we were looking for a job after the war to come to see him.

After the wedding, I was sent back to England and was posted to a bomber station called Hamstead Norris. I was in an all-RAF crew on a Stirling Bomber, and we were extremely lucky to survive during operations. We received a few flak holes on some of the trips. I remember one night, however, when we were hit by German fighters, and we had an engine shot out. We managed to cross the English Channel, and we landed on the first landing strip we could find.

When I returned to Canada in 1946, I remembered the time I toured a power plant and what the president of the company had said. I took him up on his offer, and I was the only one of the group of airmen who did. I was hired, and after a time, I became the manager of a power plant just outside of Nelson.

I have absolutely no regrets about leaving England. I had more opportunities in this country than I would have had back in the U.K. Sadly, Marjorie passed away a few years ago. We had three children—a son and two daughters. I am now retired and living in Castlegar, British Columbia, with my second wife, Lucy.

Note: I was sad to learn that Bob died on November 7, 2005, shortly after my interview with him. I talked to his widow, Lucy, and she added the following information to Bob's story.

Bob was a widower for eleven years after Marjorie's death. Bob and I had known each other for some time, and we were married on August 26, 2000, in Castlegar. Our life together for only five short years was a very happy one. He was my sweetheart.

Bob had always been very active in community life. He joined No. 581 Squadron Castlegar Air Cadets in 1954 and became commanding officer in 1955. During his time as commanding officer, the Castlegar Squadron had the honour of being the top squadron in Canada in 1968. Bob retired from the Air Cadets in 1977 with the rank of major, but remained involved with the organization until 2003. Bob was also a member of the Rotary Club, the Kiwanis, the Royal Canadian Legion, and the United Way. He served on the school board and the city council, and delivered meals on wheels for forty-four years. He and Marjorie were honoured as Castlegar's "Citizens of the Year" in 1975.

Lucy MacBain, December 2005

ERIC MARSH

MILL BAY, BRITISH COLUMBIA

My father was in the British army and was stationed in Khirkee, India, where I was born on January 21, 1922. Because war appeared to be a certainty, my friends and I joined the Bedfordshire Yeomanry, a field artillery regiment. After the Battle of Britain, the RAF needed young men to train as aircrew. I applied and was accepted.

I completed my ground training at Scarborough and qualified soon after in Carlisle as a potential pilot by flying solo in the de Havilland Tiger Moth. The next phase would take place overseas in Canada. We boarded the MV *Batory* in May 1942. In Halifax, ladies from various organizations supplied us with food that we hadn't seen in ages. We boarded the train again for the longest ride any of us had ever experienced. We had no idea

Eric and Jean Marsh during their honeymoon.
(Photo: Marsh Family)

were we were headed, but we enjoyed the journey through Ontario with its endless lakes, rocks and trees. We could hardly believe there could be so much open space on the Prairies. No wonder this place was chosen to train young men to fly.

We stopped at Congress, a small village just north of Assiniboia, Saskatchewan. This was No. 34 EFTS. Upon successfully completing this part of our training in August 1942, we were all given a forty-eight-hour leave. My friend, Jim Hyland, and I boarded the train to Moose Jaw. In River Park, Jim and I enjoyed our day swimming and eating ice cream.

While there, I noticed a young lady with a female friend sunbathing, and I had this compulsion to introduce myself. After I mentioned my intentions to Jim, he told me I was crazy, and that I would certainly get my face slapped. I said that I would have to take that chance, and I walked over and sat down on the sand. As both girls looked at me, I asked, "Would you mind if I sat here to speak with you for a minute?" They agreed, and one of them said that I didn't look like a wolf. The term, wolf, was unknown to us and never used by young English lads. I asked, "What is a wolf?" Both girls smiled and let that one go. After several minutes of polite conversation, we established our names. I asked what they were doing that evening, and I made sure to include both of them in my question, treading warily. Apparently, they were both going to the Moose Jaw Fair. I asked if they would

Eric and Jean Marsh
on their wedding day.
(Photo: Marsh Family)

mind if my friend and I tagged along. After establishing the rendezvous time, I joined Jim. My buddy wasn't the least bit interested in going to the fair, although I am positive he would have been delighted to accompany Jean instead of me.

I went to the fair by myself, and met Jean Bull and her friend. Ten minutes later, it started to rain cats and dogs, and I suggested that we see a movie. I paid for both of them since I was the one who had suggested going in the first place. Cash was always in short supply, but at a time like that, there had to be a sacrifice.

After the movie, I walked Jean home. We talked continually, and by the time we got to her house, I knew I had developed a strong rapport with her and felt that she reciprocated. I wanted to see her again, but knew the future was in the hands of the gods, since our next postings would soon be decided. I could end up hundreds of miles away, but there was a chance that I could be going to No. 32 SFTS in Moose Jaw.

Meanwhile, Jim was more than a little annoyed with my desertion during our leave together, and he had informed all our mutual friends of my behaviour. I must confess that he was right, but I felt an overwhelming need to maintain contact with this young lady. Fortunately, I was posted to No. 32 SFTS. I phoned Jean about my

Moose Jaw posting and, lucky me, she was as pleased as I was.

For the next four months, I would be in Moose Jaw becoming a potential fighter pilot while I courted this young lady. About our third or fourth date, Jean mentioned that she would be going back to school. She had a summer job at a soda fountain. I inquired whether that meant the University of Saskatchewan in Saskatoon, to which she said, "No." I then asked if she was going to Regina, and again she said, "No." She finally told me that she was returning to Central High School in Moose Jaw! After my head stopped spinning, I asked how old she was. When she told me she was sixteen, I asked myself what I was doing dating a schoolgirl. Remember, I was twenty years old at that time and the four plus years seemed completely incompatible, particularly when I thought she was eighteen or nineteen. Jean wondered what was wrong with me. After an attitude adjustment, I accepted the age difference as meaningless and, over the next several months, I became completely absorbed with this young lady.

During the next several weeks, I took every opportunity to see Jean. This had no impact on my flight training, but it did affect my ground school studies. During my previous postings, I had averaged 92% in ground school subjects. At my final exams in Moose Jaw, I averaged 75% with a 54% in navigation, a tough subject to be sure, but pretty bad. Luckily, this low mark in navigation was not too detrimental for fighter pilot training, and I received my wings and a commission on December 18, 1942.

My next posting was for pilot instruction training at Trenton, Ontario. I reluctantly had to leave Jean on January 3, 1943. The temperature was minus forty degrees, which didn't make parting any easier. We would get back together again, since I was going to instruct on Harvards at Weyburn, Saskatchewan, after completing instructor training.

It so happened that I ran into the usual military snafu at Trenton. There were five too many singles pilots in this particular course, and I was one of the pilots selected to return to the U.K. for further training. I left Canada and Jean, and all further contact between us was by mail for more than three years.

Throughout the next year, I underwent further training at No. 5 Advanced Flying Unit on Miles Masters, Marks I, II, and III. Then, I went on to No. 59 Operational Training Unit on Hawker Hurricanes, then to No. 559 Training Squadron and, finally, to No. 1 Tactical Exercise Unit.

My transfer to No. 1 Fighter Squadron took place at the beginning of December 1943. This squadron operated out of Lympne, Kent, where we flew Hawker Typhoons. In the middle of April 1944, we were transferred to North Weald and were re-equipped with Spitfires (Mark IX).

The bombardment of London by flying bombs called doodlebugs [V1s] launched from occupied territory started in June 1944. No. 165 and No. 1 Squadrons operated as a wing during this period, and because both squadrons were equipped with Spitfire IXs that were upgraded to twenty-five pounds boost, supercharge, we were considered fast enough to catch doodlebugs. We were transferred to No. 11 Group at Detling, Kent. For the next several weeks, we intercepted these little buzzers. Our squadron managed to shoot down fifty, of which I accounted for three. By early August, we were withdrawn from Flying Bomb Interceptions and resumed other offensive operations over the Continent.

Jean always wrote three times a week. I reciprocated with a letter every week to ten days on average. I dated other girls, of course, and had a jolly time on my leaves. Nevertheless, there was always that spiritual connection with that beautiful Canadian girl so many thousands of miles away. In those years, with primitive communications and vast distances, it seemed highly improbable that we would ever see each other again. However, hope is eternal, and during the summer of 1944, I purchased an engagement ring. I mailed it to her with a request that her father place it on her finger on July 26, Jean's eighteenth birthday, and he did.

Towards the end of 1944, the British were developing plans to expand their fighting forces in Southeast Asia. The end of the war in Europe was in sight, and the offensive against the Japanese in Burma was progressing well. I was transferred to No. 132, City of Bombay Squadron. We set sail for Bombay on December 14, 1944, aboard the *Queen of Bermuda*.

It was at this time that Jean decided to write on a daily basis, and there were approximately thirty airmail letters waiting for me in Bombay. She was a wonderful writer, and I can testify to her skill, which did wonders for my morale.

The squadron was sent from Bombay to Vavuniya in Ceylon. In May 1945, we were re-equipped with Spitfires, Mark XIVs—the latest version at that time for Operation Zipper. This operation was to be the invasion of Malaya, followed by the re-taking of Singapore. In June 1945, we were sent to Madura, India, and joined No. 17 Squadron for the operation. I should mention that we were considered to be seventy-five per cent expendable for Operation Zipper. In other words, three-quarters of us were not expected to survive.

About March 1945, Jean wrote to tell me that there was a possibility she could get over to the United Kingdom, but there were certain provisions. One of these was for me to submit a letter confirming my intentions to marry her whenever I returned home. I, of course, complied and, in September 1945, Jean crossed the Atlantic. She lived with my mother and sister until I returned home.

Atomic bombs were dropped in Japan in August of 1945, thus ending the war. As a result, plans for Operation Zipper were revised. Seven pilots, including myself, were transferred to No. 17 Squadron. We flew off the escort carrier, the HMS *Trumpeter* and landed at Kelenang Airstrip. After making a number of low-level sweeps around the country "showing the flag" to the defeated Japanese forces, we moved to Kuala Lumpur and repeated the sweeps there. Next, we moved to Tengah Airfield on Singapore Island, and then to Seletar Airfield bordering the Johore Bahru Strait.

Since I had served in the forces since September 1, 1939, I had a very low demobilization number, which entitled me to return to England. I arrived in England on February 16, 1946. I was demobilized the following day.

Jean met me at the front door of my mother's house. We were married in St. Margaret's Church in Bedford on February 28, 1946. Jean was nineteen and I was twenty-four.

We all know that war changes people, and I had difficulty settling down to life in England. I loved Canada and had a strong affinity for Canadians. We, therefore, moved to Canada in May of 1947.

I worked for the Canadian Pacific Railway for thirty-five years and retired to Vancouver Island in 1983. We had two girls and two boys. Jean and I will be celebrating our sixtieth wedding anniversary on February 28, 2006. Jean is seventy-nine and I am eight-four. Finally, I have to say that we still love each other and will continue to do so until death do us part.

November 2005

Alan (Al) Martin

NEPEAN, ONTARIO

When a friend lent me his copy of *Airforce Magazine*, Winter 2005–2006, I read with interest a request for information about war grooms. I was one, although called a male war bride in our family.

I was born in London on May 19, 1921, and, at the outbreak of the war, I was an apprentice in an engineering firm making cockpit canopies for several types of aircraft. It was a reserved occupation, and one could not be called up, nor could one quit or change jobs, other than volunteering as a submariner or as aircrew. I chose the latter and began my RAF service career on March 23, 1942. In January 1943, I was posted overseas to complete my training.

I arrived in Canada in a blinding snowstorm, but after crossing the Atlantic in a ship designed, I believe, for tropical waters, even the dock at Halifax looked great. However, the real wonder and beauty of the land really hit me when we arrived in Moncton. It was a clear, cold night with fresh snow everywhere, and there was that incredible hush that follows a winter storm. It was truly a picture-book setting among the dark and snow-draped trees. There were lights everywhere, warm barracks with lots of hot water, and apple pie with ice cream at the YMCA. "What a wonderful world," as Louis Armstrong was to sing.

Al and Barbara Martin on their wedding day.
(Photo: Martin Family)

I was a product of the BCATP. From Moncton, I went to Picton, Ontario, for bombing and gunnery training, then to St. Jean, Quebec, for training in navigation, and then on to No. 34 OTU at Penfield

Ridge, New Brunswick. This OTU provided training in low-level, daylight, intruder flying and tactics. I was somewhat surprised to be posted from there to Ferry Command where, shortly thereafter, I was at 10,000 feet in a B24 heading for Prestwick, Scotland, in the dead of night. Career planning it wasn't, but ours was "not to reason why." Besides, who would complain about life in Montreal? Not I!

In 1944, I was based at Dorval. As there was no station there in the usual sense, we found our own accommodation in Montreal. When not away on trips, I spent the occasional afternoon or evening at a service club on Sherbrooke Street called Airforce House. It was a big, old, stately home, and it was there where I met a tall, slim, and lovely girl with red-gold hair. We talked, and I learned that her name was Barbara Ann Gardham. She was a nurse in training at a local hospital. Although she worked twelve-hour shifts, she was a volunteer hostess at the club when time permitted.

That night, I went back to my rented room quite sure I had met the girl I wanted to marry. She, I learned much later, was much less certain. Barbara loved to dance, and she quickly found out that I had two left feet. We were off to a bad start, but we met from time to time and, one day, I was invited to dinner at her house. Her parents were friendly, but I imagine they were thinking, "Well, whom has she brought to supper this time?" I seemed to fit in, however, and Barbara's dad, who had a schooner at a yacht club near Montreal, was glad to have a deckhand able to do a bit of wood-working and engine maintenance, and a lot of hull-painting and caulking! Between working, nursing, and flying, we all had some great times sailing and swimming. Her mum, too, soon had me on the end of a shovel in her Victory Garden.

On April 21, 1945, left feet were forgiven, and we were married, a week later than planned, as the newspaper announcement said, "due to the exigencies of war." Actually, on the 14th, I was steaming into New York on the *Queen Elizabeth* after a U.K. delivery, and my best man was in a C47 somewhere between Cairo and Karachi. My parents could not attend the ceremony, of course, as they were 3,000 miles away, preoccupied with air raids, blackouts, shortages of just about everything, and other day-to-day details of wartime living. They were cool to the news of our engagement and subsequent marriage, images, perhaps, of log cabins, wolves, bears and Grey Owl! Their perceptions changed when Barbara came to England and, after my father's death, when Mother came to stay with us for one winter.

When the war was over, I returned to the U.K. in the fall of 1945, thinking that I would soon be demobilized and back to Canada in a few months. The RAF, however, thought otherwise. I was kept busy helping to bring service personnel back from the Far East, and in 1947, Barbara came over to sample England's austerity. It wasn't until January 1948 that we set foot in Canada again, arriving at the famous Pier 21 in Halifax. Barbara was a returning Canadian, and I was a landed immigrant.

We lived with Barbara's parents at their peach farm in Grimsby, Ontario, but I was restless, and the following year, I was back in the air again with the RCAF Search and Rescue K Flight at Edmonton. In the years that followed, we, like all service families, moved around the country at the whim of those green signals that arrived from Air Transport Command Headquarters and Air Force Headquarters.

I retired from the RCAF after reaching compulsory retirement age. We continue to live in Ottawa, as do our two sons, their wives and our two grandsons.

We have returned many times to England and have taken our two boys over to meet their cousins and to experience the beauty of the English countryside, the taste of fresh fried fish and chips in a village street, and real ale in ancient inns. We like to visit, but I have no thoughts of moving there. Canada is home.

Very soon, Barbara and I will celebrate our sixty-first wedding anniversary, and as I look back, I realize that we have indeed been fortunate. We have not been without some dark times. There were separations, worries about children and parents, and occasional ill health, but we have made a good life together, and I look back with affection to that old and stately home on Sherbrooke Street where so much of it began.

March 2006

KENNETH MCDONALD

NORTH YORK, ONTARIO

The following story is based on Ken's autobiography, A Wind on the Heath: A Memoir.

I was one of seven RAF pilots posted to Canada to help start the British Commonwealth Air Training Plan. We sailed from Southampton on August 19, 1939, and reached Montreal on August 26. [From there, we were flown to Trenton and arrived on a Sunday afternoon.] The mess was crowded with cheerful officers, their wives or girlfriends, all joining in the kind of welcome Canadians are noted for. We were impressed.

Four days later, Desmond McGlinn and I were posted to Camp Borden. In an effort to get the most out of a limited number of aircraft and instructors, we worked twenty-four hours on and twenty-four hours off. One shift would hand over to the next at midday, when the shift that was relieved would rest for twenty-four hours. Instead, as soon as we had eaten lunch on the days off, we piled into cars, and headed south for Toronto and the Royal York Hotel, where the fourth floor [was] set aside for the RCAF.

Borden's airfield was grass, as were those we had flown from in England, and when the snow came, it was compacted with rollers, a typically practical Canadian approach to the local conditions in that heavy snowbelt. The bush pilots who came through for refresher

Ken and Ruth McDonald on their wedding day.
(Photo: McDonald Family)

Ken and Ruth McDonald on their wedding day.
(Photo: McDonald Family)

training were older and, in many cases, had more flying experience than we did. When Ansons arrived at Borden, I used them as flying classrooms. The bush pilots would take it in turns as first pilot. It was the accepted drill that when we were on finals, the navigators would run back and forth in the cabin to change the trim for the man in the left-hand seat, battling with the control column.

The first few weeks were filled with a sense of foreignness, combined with kinship, and a daily realization of how practical and down-to-earth Canadians were. [We were impressed with the] expertise and management capabilities of the entrepreneurs who ran the civilian-operated schools that played such a major part in the success of the whole training effort.

The town nearest to Borden was Barrie, where I met Ruth Margaret Craig on a blind date in September, courtesy of Jean Lay who ran The Flower Bar. Its back room was a rendezvous for many of the instructors.

Ruth and I got on well from the start, became engaged in February 1940, and were married on May 17. That is sixty-five years ago as I write, but I can recapture it as if it were yesterday. The excitement centred on the young, fair-haired woman who always seemed glad to see me. [Her] eyes lit up when I made her laugh, and [she] made me laugh in turn. She exuded an air of calmness, and yet was game for any of the activities that turned up, usually at short notice.

Ruth's father found us a ground-floor flat in the Bayview Apartments, a sister-in-law helped us get furniture together, and we were there for four months until I was posted to Trenton for the specialist navigation course. A month later, the navigation school was moved about 1,500 miles west to Rivers, Manitoba.

When the course ended eight weeks later, I was posted to Regina. Ruth went house-hunting, and within a day or two, had us installed in a second-floor corner flat in the new Grenfell Apartments. Our three-month stay at Regina was average for that period of the war when airfields were being opened up across the country.

Our move from there to Portage la Prairie was a lucky one, just over a year in duration. My job was chief supervisory officer of the No. 7 Air Observer School. Cy Becker, an Edmonton lawyer who had been a fighter pilot in World War I, was the manager, Matt Berry the operations manager, Scotty Moir the chief pilot, and Rex Terpenning the engineer. They and their civilian staff flew and maintained the Ansons and looked after the infrastructure without any fuss, but with great efficiency. That was the spirit I remember from those days in Canada: getting on with things without a lot of fuss. As I look back on them now, the airfields, aircraft, and all that went into them, were tremendous achievements.

Mother wrote regularly, but didn't say much about the bombing except that it was a nuisance and made jokes about huddling under the stairs for safety. In the last letter she wrote on June 21, 1942, which caught up with me after we left Portage, she must have known she had cancer, but said little about herself.

[Before I was posted to the U.K. to serve with Bomber Command, Ruth and I] were in Montreal for the month of June while I converted to the Hudson. Ruth found us a room we could afford in Mme. Trudel's house on Bishop Street, saw me off every morning in the scheduled bus that left Dominion Square for Dorval, and spent her days pretty much alone until I came back in the late afternoon. On July 8, 1942, after a forlorn parting with Ruth in Dominion Square, I flew a Ventura to Prestwick [Scotland], spent a few days leave with Mother and her sister in Southampton. [I was] was not long at OTU when Mother died on August 14, 1942.

Our crew consisted of three Canadians, three Englishmen, and a Scot. From Pershore OTU, we flew Wellingtons to Bremen and Essen. Later from Linton, where I was OC B Flight on 78 Squadron, we flew Halifax IIs to twenty-six more targets. I was promoted to wing commander as OC, the Heavy Conversion Unit at Marston Moor. That was where Ruth joined me after a twenty-one-day passage of the Atlantic during which the convoy lost three ships.

For Ruth, the four years from July 1942 to May 1946, were a blend of loneliness and frustration while she was waiting in Canada and then in England. Peter was born in York while we were there. [After various accommodations] we found Lane

End Cottage near Bury St. Edmund's where John was born.

Where and how we lived for the first dozen years of our married life is a testament to the fact that whatever talent I had was totally unsuited to the elementary duty of finding places to lay our heads; at that, I was a washout. Even during the war, when accommodation of any kind was at a premium, we might have fared a good deal better if Ruth had been doing the searching.

[When the war was over], I was posted to the RCAF College in Toronto and was flown there in a converted Liberator. Ruth got passage at very short notice on the *Stella Polaris*. It was to sail from Bergen [Norway]. Ruth and two babies made their way from Southampton across London to Newcastle for the ferry to Bergen. Several days later, I met them in New York.

When the course ended [at RCAF College], I agitated successfully for an exchange posting in RCAFHQ. [At the end of this posting], we returned to England in 1948 on the *Aquitania's* last voyage. [I was] posted to the Joint Services Staff College course near Chesham Bois. We stayed for a week at a residential hotel before renting an upstairs flat in an Elizabethan barn for the winter. The next posting was to Air Ministry. [We bought a house before Martha, our daughter, was born], and we stayed put until 1952.

After being posted to the directing staff of the RAF Staff College at Bracknell, we spent two months in a converted bus joined by a covered walkway to a caravan.

Our next posting was to Singapore. On promotion to group captain, we moved into the CO's quarter of RAF Changi. [At this point in our lives], we decided it was time to settle in Canada where we wanted the children to grow up. At the end of the tour, therefore, and on return to England in 1956, I applied to retire at my own request.

Three weeks after our return to Canada, I was lucky to get a job with Canadair in Montreal, where we stayed while the children passed through school and university. [I then became] sick of travelling and retired again. We moved to Toronto, and I started to do what I'd always wanted to do, but couldn't afford until then, namely write.

Throughout all this tale of movement and apparent instability, there was one constant: Ruth's and my love for each other. On the 17th of May, 2000, our children mounted a splendid celebration in the house and presented us with an enlargement of the wedding picture as we emerged from Collier Street United Church in Barrie, sixty years before.

But the years were beginning to tell. Ruth's long history of high blood pressure and high cholesterol, accompanied by other ailments, led to a gradual deterioration.

Despite unremitting efforts by the intensive care unit's dedicated staff, as well as Ruth's own inherent courage, the strain was too great for her, and she died at 2 p.m. on April 18, 2002.

I watched her die, watched the last laboured breath escape from the mouth already cold as I kissed it for the last time. Twenty-nine days shy of our sixty-second wedding anniversary, Ruth was no longer there. The next morning, early, when I was sitting in the armchair of this office, Ruth appeared at the door of the room, as she had done many times, but this time for a moment only, still, silent, and smiling at me.

There were so many good times. That is what we remembered when we sat on balconies looking at the sea or the woods, and that is what I remember now.

December 2005

Henry Trent McGlynn

LAKEVILLE, NEW BRUNSWICK

I will first introduce myself as a war groom of many years. I was born in Devon and brought up on the Isle of Wight and in Southampton, England. I went to war with the RAF.

I suppose one should go back in time to the British Commonwealth Air Training Plan and the Avro Anson. I was with a Coastal Command unit in the maintenance section in 1940 until the evacuation of the British Expeditionary and French forces at Dunkirk. I then took a short gunnery course. After a few interviews, I was put on the maintenance unit list and sent to the Avro factory in Chester. I spent my time stripping and disassembling the Ansons that were being sent to Canada. They were being re-assembled in Canada and used as training aircraft.

Needless to say, they also needed workers to go to Canada with knowledge of the Anson, and I was one of a crew of four that was sent. There was one engine man (me), an airframe person, an electrician, and an instrument person, as well as one corporal to keep us in line, I suppose.

On January 27, 1941, we arrived in Halifax, Nova Scotia, on the Australian ship, the *Orantes*. Soon, everyone had left the ship but we gallant four. No one knew who we were or where to send us. After freezing on the ship and experiencing the usual military snafu, we were on our way to Charlottetown, P.E.I., where we rejoined the others. There, we encountered our old Ansons again and took on the task of rebuilding them. I believe we did about eight at that time with the help of the groundcrew.

Charlottetown was a bit of a let down to us limeys. Imagine coming from England to a dry province with no pubs! There were, however, lots of dances, and we English loved to dance. At one dance above Redding's Drugstore, I met Mary, the future Mrs. Henry McGlynn. She was

Henry and Mary McGlynn on their wedding day.
(Photo: McGlynn Family)

dancing with a bloke with two left feet, and I cut in. I did find out later in our courtship that she had watched me at a few dances and had secretly wanted to dance with me. I guess she thought I was good on my feet.

The romance started that night. Mary was born in Charlottetown and lived at home with her father. Her brother was in the army and was overseas at the time. Mary was only fourteen when her mother died. I used to take the bus or a taxi from the base into town, and then return again either by bus or taxi. Her dad was quite an old-fashioned man, and I had to be out of the house by 10:00 p.m.

The Canadian winters were also quite a shock to the system. My friends and I tried to learn to ice-skate once. I guess we thought, "When in Rome, do as the Romans do." A young lady took about six of us to a bicycle shop where we bought skates, and then she took us to the Forum. I donned the skates, took one step out on to the ice and immediately fell. It wasn't as simple as it looked. We all headed back to the base and re-sold the skates.

My travels in the Service were not over. After a year, I was on the move again, and was issued a blue blazer and grey slacks. I was sent to the U.S. Passaic base in New Jersey, the home of the Pratt and Whitney engine. There, I took a six-week course, and then I was sent to Penfield Ridge, New Brunswick. It wasn't long before I was off again, this time to the Douglas Plant in San Diego, California, for about four weeks for another course. After that course ended, it was back to New Brunswick.

The whole time I was travelling, Mary and I kept in touch by mail. She travelled by train from Charlottetown to Black's Harbour, New Brunswick, and we got married on March 3, 1943. We had three days together, and then she was on her way back home. We remained married until March 15, 1999, when she died. I miss her dearly.

Not long after our marriage, I was on the move again. I was sent back to the U.K. in time for the Normandy Invasion with Transport Command. Our task was to help with glider hauling and the paratroop drop. My wife remained in Canada. It was a good job that she did because after the Invasion, I was off to Egypt to help with the transportation of ex POWs from Japanese prison camps. By Christmas 1945, I was back in the U.K. with my family. On Christmas Eve, I was demobilized, but I still had to remain in Britain for three months in case something else started up. I knew that Canada was where I wanted to spend the rest of my life.

On March 27, 1946, I boarded the *Aquitania*, and I was on my way to Canada, my wife and a new life. I arrived at Pier 21 in Halifax on April Fool's Day in 1946, and Mary was there to meet me. After days in Halifax, we went to Charlottetown.

Because Mary's father was in ill health, we lived in the same house with him.

Mary nursed him until his death in 1947. When I first arrived back in Canada, the only job I could get was peeling poles. Mary's brother, who was back from the army, worked with me. In January 1947, my employer told me that they were looking for people to work at the airport in Charlottetown, and I went for an interview. Ten days later, I went to work for Maritime Central Airways.

Here, I was in a new country, and I finally had a good job to support my wife. In April 1947, we had our first-born, a son. Canada has been good to me. I have always felt that I had more opportunities here in this country than I would ever have had in England. Canadians are not as class-conscious as the British and, therefore, people can advance according to their abilities.

The Maritime Central Airways eventually became EPA [Eastern Provincial Airways], and we were all transferred to Moncton, New Brunswick. Eventually, EPA moved its business to Halifax. By that time, our two children were married, and it was just the two of us again. In the early 1980s, EPA was bought out by CPAir. I retired in 1984 after thirty-seven years with the company. Unfortunately, not too many people in today's society can claim that they worked that many years with the same company. It is a changing world.

I have never regretted the move I made from my homeland to a new country. I started out in Canada as a pole-peeler, and by the time I retired, I was the engineering supervisor. Quite a feat! To quote an old TV commercial, "Only in Canada, you say?" I've been blessed in this country. I've been back to England over the years to visit family, but always returned home to Canada.

March 2006

NORMAN MCKEEMAN

YORKTON, SASKATCHEWAN

I was born in Cairns, North Queensland, Australia, on February 9, 1923, and grew up in the nearby town of Gordonvale. I enlisted in the RAAF in August 1941, but it was April 1942 before I got my call. I took my initial training in a de Havilland Tiger Moth in Australia. In November 1942, I came to Canada and was posted to the manning depot in Edmonton to await a posting to a more advanced flying school.

How I got to Yorkton, Saskatchewan, is an interesting story. There were about fifty or sixty of us Aussies in the drill hall in Edmonton waiting to be assigned to various service flying training schools on the Prairies. We heard one of the Canadian officers say that eight students were required to fill a course at No. 11 SFTS in Yorkton, Saskatchewan. Seven chums and I volunteered en masse for the posting and were able to stay together during our training days.

We travelled from Edmonton to Yorkton via the CNR, and we got off at the town of Melville. We made the remaining twenty miles or so by truck. This truck was of the open variety and had a tarpaulin thrown over the back. At −10 F, as one of our chaps put it, "We bloody near froze." On arrival at the station, we proceeded to the records section and were instantly warmed by the sight of a beautiful girl who was working there. A week later, we met this girl, whose name was Merle Ward, at a local dance, but this time she was accompanied by a carbon copy, her twin sister, Pearl. One of the chaps remarked, "My God, they're two of them!" It did not take us long to ask the girls to dance, and that is how I first met Pearl, who would become my wife about a year later. Pearl thought I was a pretty good dancer. We Australians danced more along the English style. We got along famously, even winning the prize for the waltz that evening.

The following weekend, I met Pearl again at the dance and, afterward, one of my Aussie pals and I were invited to her parents' home where Mrs. Ward served us a light lunch. Many of the Yorkton citizens opened their homes to the young pilot trainees, and their hospitality was especially appreciated by those of us from Britain, New Zealand and Australia. The Wards provided a warm and welcoming place for Pearl and me, and we began to see each other regularly. There were more

Norman and Pearl McKeeman on their wedding day.
(Photo: McKeeman Family)

dances and more weekends at her home until I graduated in April 1943.

Learning to fly during the winter on the Canadian Prairies was an experience. During our training, we were all so eager to get our wings that the fear of being washed out was always with us. On one occasion, I did think my flying days were over. On a solo training flight in a Cessna Crane, I was practising a single-engine approach and landing which required delaying the lowering of the undercarriage until well into the final approach. With engines throttled back and wheels retracted, warning signals and lights normally would be activated, but due to an electrical malfunction, this did not happen, and I was blissfully unaware that my wheels were still up. Fortunately, I did not land, since with the reduced drag, the aircraft would not settle and was going to overshoot the runway. I had to open throttles to go around for another approach and landing. On doing so, I reached for the undercarriage switch, and to my horror, found it still in the up position. My commanding officer took a dim view of this oversight and, as a punishment, I was confined to barracks for fourteen days. Had I landed and wrecked the aircraft, I certainly would have been washed out.

The people in Yorkton were so kind and hospitable, and although the Aussies were sometimes considered a rowdy lot, we felt that it was our responsibility to behave properly, and we did. We were well regarded by the local citizens, and the feeling was mutual. During my training days in Yorkton, and the times I came back on weekends, I got to know many of the local people well. When I did come back for good, it was easy to call Yorkton home.

Following graduation, I had expected to be posted overseas to Britain but, instead, I was chosen to be an instructor, and was sent to the flying instructors' school at Vulcan, Alberta, for a two-month training course. Afterwards, I was posted to the flying school at Dauphin, Manitoba, to commence my instructing duties. None of us were particularly happy about becoming instructors, but I did not mind because Dauphin is only about 100 miles east of Yorkton, and I was able to return there on weekends. By this time, Pearl and I had become serious about our relationship. I scraped up $50, and, with the kindness of a Yorkton jeweller, was able to purchase a reasonably decent engagement ring. I proposed to Pearl while sharing a Coke float in a restaurant on Broadway Street. We were married on Saturday, the 6th of November, 1943, in Holy Trinity Anglican Church in Yorkton.

Our first home was in Dauphin, and it certainly was not a palace. Accommodation was very scarce during wartime, but we were able to rent two rooms in the private home of an elderly couple. Another air force couple and their daughter stayed there too, and we were a wee bit crowded. Our rooms consisted of half of the downstairs living room converted to a bedroom and a room upstairs which served as our sitting room and kitchen. We cooked on a coal oil stove, and shared a bathroom with the others. Were we unhappy? Not on your life! We thought it was heaven.

Early in 1944, I was posted back to Vulcan, Alberta, and we were able to find a very comfortable apartment in the town of Nanton, just a few miles west of the station. We liked Nanton, as it was a very friendly town. We made many great friends there.

In December 1944, I learned that I was to be posted to Australia. Pearl, who was expecting our first child, returned to Yorkton where I joined her a short time later to enjoy a short leave before leaving for the Pacific. I was actually on the final days of this embarkation leave when Pearl went into labour. I sent a telegram requesting an extension and was given two more days which enabled me to be present at the birth of Merle, named after Pearl's twin sister, on January 29, 1945. I had to leave the very next day and, a few weeks later, I was back in Australia where I resumed my flying duties. I was discharged from the service in October 1945. Meanwhile, arrangements were made for Pearl and baby Merle to arrive in Sydney about the same time.

We resided in Brisbane, and I went back to my old job with the Forestry Department. We struggled along for about two years, and then I got the notion to move on. I had always enjoyed my time in Canada and considered it a very progressive country. Pearl was surprised and delighted by my decision. We arrived back in Yorkton in January 1948.

Pearl's dad owned a greenhouse that he operated almost by himself. I joined the business to help out and to learn something about horticulture. The greenhouse was situated in the residential region of Yorkton, but a florist shop in the downtown area was needed. When I had learned enough about the business, we opened up Yorkton Florists Ltd. in 1949. I eventually bought Mr. Ward's shares and operated the business until the 1990s when I retired and turned the business over to my eldest son.

My parents visited us in 1958 and thought they would stay for a couple of months. However, in order to stay that long, my dad had to have some kind of employment. Dad was an accountant and got a good job with a local car dealership. My parents both liked Yorkton and Canada so much that they decided to stay permanently. My older brother had died in 1939, and I was essentially an only child. With our kids being their only grandchildren, it was not difficult for them to sever ties with Australia, and they were delighted when we named one of our sons after my deceased brother. They both lived until their late eighties and never regretted their decision to stay in Canada.

While in business, I felt I owed something to the community that had welcomed me as a young airman and as a young businessman. I was a member of the high school board for fourteen years, serving as chairman for eight of those years. I served as president of the Yorkton Chamber of Commerce, as well as president of the Canadian Legion and was zone commander. I am a past master of the masonic lodge and a past president of the Kinsmen Club. I was also on the committee for the air cadets and served on the provincial executive.

Our first trip back to Australia was in 1983, and I renewed contact with a good number of my cousins as well as old school chums and air force friends. We make a point of keeping in touch regularly, and several have visited us in Yorkton. Pearl and I made another trip back in 1997 when we attended the hundredth anniversary of my old elementary school and, again, renewed friendships.

We have three girls and two boys, fifteen grandchildren and two great-grandchildren. I have no regrets about coming to Canada. I am almost eighty-three now, and I wake up in the morning and look forward to the day. Life has been good.

February 2006

JACK MEADOWS

WHITE ROCK, BRITISH COLUMBIA

In the fall of 1940, June, the twenty-year-old daughter of a Prince Rupert doctor was in the U.S. at the University of Washington studying home economics. However, Canadian wartime foreign exchange controls meant she had to transfer to a Canadian university. She chose Macdonald College, part of Montreal's McGill University. The different syllabus meant that she had to attend summer school at the University of Manitoba in 1941 before entering Macdonald College in the fall.

In that autumn of 1940, I was an RAF flying officer, celebrating my twenty-first birthday at the Randolph Hotel in Oxford, England. It was a depressing occasion. I was already disgruntled because, having already been flying for three years, I had been made an instructor, and had spent the Battle of Britain teaching others how to fight. I was now disgusted by the news that I had to go to Canada, which meant even more delay before getting to a Spitfire squadron. I did not realize at the time that this posting probably saved my life.

Among new friends posted to Canada with me were a number of Canadians who had gone to England before the war to join the RAF. Even they did not know the exact location of Carberry, Manitoba, my new posting. More importantly, however, these fellows inducted their British pals into Canadian habits and customs. Knowledge of strange liquor laws was invaluable. At each stop on the three-day dry, train journey from Halifax to Winnipeg, they showed us how to grab a cab and use the one-hour wait to rush to the nearest government liquor store for beer.

It was November and I had the shock of a Canadian prairie winter. While we were in Brandon to buy fur hats, five of us visited a beer parlour. The Canadians explained to the ignorant Brits that standing was not allowed, as it was in British pubs, and that the salt shakers on each table were used to flatten the fizz of the weak, over-aerated beer. A Canadian automatically said to the barman, "Five beers."

The barman asked me how old I was. At that time, I looked about eighteen. "Twenty-one," I replied, "Why do you ask?"

He then asked the same question of Bob, two years an officer, with as big a bar bill as anyone. Bob had already been decorated with a Distinguished Flying Cross and was on a rest from operations. "Twenty," he answered.

"You're too young. I can't serve you," the barman said. Our Canadian pals erupted. A compromise was reached with two large jugs of beer and an extra glass. Another lesson learned!

As Carberry was far from ready, a number of us were seconded to a new RCAF station at Macleod, Alberta, which at that early stage of the tremendous British Commonwealth Air Training Plan had no instructors. The aeroplanes had to be ferried to Macleod from Winnipeg, however, and we got to know much more of Canada and its kind and generous people in both places. They overlooked our brashness and treated us as battle heroes. It was very embarrassing for those of us who had been instructing the whole time. By the time we got back to Carberry, we Brits had been well indoctrinated into Canadian customs, habits, and history.

Carberry's officers decided to give a big ball at the summer solstice of 1941 to thank all those from as far away as Winnipeg for their kindness. I had met a number of nice girls from Winnipeg, but none I especially wanted to ask out, nor did I know how to solve the problem of getting them the hundred or so miles to and from Carberry. My new friend, a little older and much more experienced than I, asked a girl he had met who was studying at the University of Manitoba Summer School. He arranged for her to stay with another friend and his wife in Carberry.

June was tall with long blonde hair, slim in a close-fitting seersucker dress, and I fell at once in love. I danced almost every dance with her. Any conscience about stealing a friend's girl was quickly dulled by the knowledge that he had a wife in England. Every weekend I could get away was spent in Winnipeg courting her. A great shortage of instructors meant that I was also flying twice the proper amount and verging on a breakdown. Just as June was returning home to Prince Rupert, I was ordered away for a rest and went with her on the train as far as Jasper. I was half miserable and half glad that she did not ask me to go on. Obviously, she was not ready to introduce me to her family.

I saw June briefly in Winnipeg on her journey east to Montreal in the fall. Telephoning was still expensive and difficult over long distances, apart from the time difference, but we wrote copiously. Then, I got an unexpected call from her mother. June must have said enough about me to worry her mother who wanted to make sure that a foreigner existed. At least on the phone, I sounded reasonably civilized. I did not then understand why she called for what was an awkward chat about nothing in particular.

Due for proper leave, I wrote to June saying I would come to Montreal and asked her to marry me. She said, "Yes." June told her parents that she and I were going to Sainte-Adéle to ski and did not mention marriage. As a precaution, her worried mother got June's seventeen-year-old-brother, who was at college at Toronto, to come with us instead of going home for Christmas. Thankfully, he was a poor chaperon. We somehow ditched him and went back to Montreal to ask the Catholic church to marry us. It laughed at us! At St. George's Anglican Church, the archdeacon asked if our parents knew, and we said that they didn't. "Who are your witnesses?" We got the cab driver and the cleaning lady. "Where's your hat?" he asked June who had none. "Dear me, what would St. Paul say?" Then, he married us.

June came back to Winnipeg again for summer school in 1942, and we took a tiny flat there. Later, we lived in a trailer in a Carberry back garden. After the wedding, I broke the news to my parents, and June, eventually, faced doing the same to hers. The only recrimination from June's family was that there had been no Roman Catholic ceremony. In July, June went home, and in September, I got leave. By then I was at RCAF Vulcan, Alberta. I went out to Prince Rupert for a better reception from June's family than was deserved. The original wedding was kept quiet, since the RC church did not recognize it. "What would the neighbours think?" After I had a row with an unpleasant, young Irish priest whose supposed Catholic indoctrination of Protestant Jack consisted entirely of slanging June for her behaviour, it went well, and almost at once, we were on the train back to Vulcan. June lived at first in Calgary, where I visited every weekend, and later, she stayed in the little Vulcan Hotel. Early in 1943, I was posted to Trenton, Ontario. June stayed with an aunt in Belleville until we found an apartment in a Trenton house. In March, I was posted back to the U.K. I had been a war groom for just over a year.

We both knew my suggestion of a quick return to Canada was false pretense, so June applied for a passage to England which came through in September. June was, by then, indoctrinated in British habits to some extent, and this helped to ease the shock of Britain at its lowest ebb, with its rationing, shortages, restrictions, and blackouts. The law said she must do war work. June joined the U.S. Red Cross, and I flew in my Spitfire to visit her. Then, I went night-fighting, and for a while we (she full time, me on alternate two nights when not flying) lived in a terrible, cold, damp labourer's cottage two miles from my Yorkshire base. Soon after the Invasion when I was in France, June went to live with my parents, and somehow managed to cope with a strange English mother-in-law and local customs.

We never seriously considered returning to Canada after the war. June nobly followed me around London, Edinburgh, and back to London. Eventually, with two daughters, we left for South Africa in 1957. Back in England in 1965, we lived in London, Suffolk, and Brighton, and made many trips around Europe. In 1981 after thirty-five years with Unilever, I retired, and the big question was where to live.

June was almost completely anglicized at that point. In 1950, she had been back to Canada for two months. In 1977 as a family, we had a two-week visit in B.C. Apart from that, neither of us had been to Canada since 1943. However, both our daughters were, for complicated reasons, living in Vancouver at that time, and we decided to go there, neither of us believing it would be permanent. After we made the decision to stay in Canada, I had to satisfy the authorities that I would not be a burden on the state, that I was healthy, and that I did not have TB or syphilis. On April 1, 1981, we were in Vancouver. I was now a landed immigrant sponsored by my wife. Once again, and after thirty-eight years, I was a war groom.

No house we viewed satisfied June. Then, we saw an almost completed new house on a builder's acre on the borders of Surrey and White Rock in British Columbia. I thought it was too big for us in retirement and had too much land. I sat opposite June and our daughters and was hammered by all three. Finally, I agreed, provided that June never, ever complain that the house was too much work. She never has, even now in our late eighties.

So, we are still here. For a couple of years I was the part-time director of the short-lived Grape and Wine Institute of B.C. while creating a garden out of the bare lot around the house. Time allowed me to play golf again, and eventually, I became president of my little local club. I played an active part in the Canadian Museum of Flight and in various air force associations. As soon as possible, I became a Canadian citizen. "At least I don't have to check your knowledge of English," said the judge as she put me through the rest of the inquisition.

More importantly, I had started serious writing. First, it was a family history, and then I wrote many articles regularly published by aviation magazines. There were also books, one about Canada's great Commonwealth Air Training Plan. The story of my first spell as a war groom was based on my letters home and to June, and also on a 1986 trip we made across Canada revisiting the places concerned. It was, I thought, an interesting social history. The book was acclaimed by editors who said, and still do, that the potential market was too small. In 1990, they said wait ten years; in 2005 they said it was ten years too late. One said that there is not enough blood, guts and flying; another said too much.

Meanwhile, June is very much a homebody. She has outside interests in garden clubs, hospital auxiliaries, and nearby relatives who are younger than we are, and are, sadly, dying off. She worries too much about our daughters and grandson, but she enjoys cruising. Most years, we have visited the U.K. We have now been in this house for twenty-five years. We dread the possible need in due course, perhaps

A graduating class from No. 33 SFTS celebrate in Winnipeg.
(Photo: Commonwealth Air Training Plan Museum)

in our nineties, to have to downsize. What is particularly interesting is that while the war groom is very well adjusted here, and has no wish to move anywhere else, his Canadian-born wife is the one who is homesick for England. Granted, it is the England she knew thirty years or so ago, rather different to the England of today. Sixty-five years of marriage have made irrelevant St. Paul's dicta on hats.

May 2006

Jack Meredith

STRATFORD, PRINCE EDWARD ISLAND

*Jack and Bernice Meredith
on their wedding day.*
(Photo: Meredith Family)

I was born in Heywood, Lancashire. I worked in a cotton mill after I left school, but I didn't like the noise and the smell. In 1938, Jim Hilton and I went to Manchester to join the RAF when we were both nineteen. Jim's mother blamed me for talking him into joining up, and my mother blamed Jim for the same thing.

After basic training, it was on to wireless school in Yatesbury, Wiltshire. I also learned how to fire a machine gun from an airplane and how to do maintenance work on aircraft.

In 1939, I was sent to France with the British Expeditionary Force, and while I was there, I flew about a dozen sorties in support of the ground troops. When we got the word that we had to evacuate, we destroyed all the planes that couldn't fly. The ones that could fly, took off, loaded with VIPs, and the rest of us packed up our seventeen trucks, each one hauling a trailer. As we headed for the coast, German Stukas [dive-bombers] played hell with us, and we lost more men and trucks each day. When we got to Le Havre, we smashed the radio equipment in the seven remaining trucks, drove them to the top of the cliffs, and pushed them over. We were able to board a ship after we helped unload ammunition for the British Army, and we arrived safely back in England with only the clothes on our backs.

I was then sent to a navigation training unit at Squire's Gate, just outside of Blackpool. Because training stations in England were vulnerable to bombing, many of them were transferred to Canada as part of the British Commonwealth Air Training Plan.

I was one of the hundreds of airmen sent to Canada to staff these training schools. After boarding at Greenock, Scotland, we learned that we were headed for Canada, a place of polar bears, Indians, and a wolf around each corner. That was our perception at the time.

The twelve-day crossing was terrible. Morale was low because the ship was a stinking mess, and there was nothing to do. We spent our time playing cards, strolling the deck, and watching the *Royal Sovereign*, our escort, sail around us. The lights in Halifax Harbour were a welcome sight for those of us who had just come from a land of blackouts.

RAF personnel were sent all over Canada, and I ended up in Charlottetown, Prince Edward Island. When we first arrived on the Island, we had a four-mile walk to the training station that was still under construction. We soon learned, to our dismay, that Prince Edward Island had one hundred per cent prohibition, and there was no place to buy a bottle of beer except from the bootleggers. After a month, all the bootleggers were declared out of bounds to the troops. At this point, morale was pretty low, since the base was still unfinished, and there was nothing set up for us. Eventually, things got better once the buildings were up and supplies started to come in.

Our Avro Ansons had been taken apart in England and were re-assembled at the base. During that winter, some of the boys had the tedious job of opening and closing the hangar doors several times a day to prevent the rollers from freezing. I made two or three flights a day teaching navigation to airmen who were destined for Coastal or Bomber Command.

After the base was established, we had all kinds of entertainment, such as dances, plays, and concerts. We talked the sports officer into putting in a hockey rink at the base, even though many of us had never even been on skates. Some of the boys learned to play hockey and challenged a female team from Charlottetown called the Abbie Sisters. Almost every time an Englishman knocked down one of the Abbie Sisters, he stopped his play to help her get back on her feet. Needless to say, the Abbie Sisters won!

I recall another incident that happened after we arrived in Canada. Ronson lighters were just coming into the stores and were quite the rage at the time. Some of the boys discovered an ingenious way to refill them. An overflow section in the wing of the Anson carried gasoline. If one went to the tip of the wing and shook it up and down, one would get a little gasoline from the overflow tube at the tip. One day, an airman shook the end of the wing, and some of the gasoline splashed onto his hands. He flipped the lighter on, and you can imagine what happened next! The plane had a little damage, but the airman's hands were severely burned.

Naturally, we tried to spend as much time as possible in Charlottetown when on leave. There was a skating rink, two movie theatres, and several dance halls. Nearby Brackley Beach became a popular place for the airmen. Three of us bought an old Studebaker that wouldn't run and had it towed to the base. We fixed it up, and it carried eight to ten of us out to Brackley Beach for enjoyable outings.

It was legal for those of us in the military to drive service vehicles without a license, but I knew I should have a driver's license for the car. I drove to the RCMP barracks on Upper Prince Street to get one. A constable brought out the forms, asked me some questions and said, "Sign there." My buddy tried the same thing, but he had to deal with the superintendent who charged him $10 for driving the car into town without a license.

On long cross-country flights, I had been allowed to take over the controls of the Anson to get the feel of the plane in case an emergency ever arose. In early 1942, while on a flight over New Brunswick in poor weather, the pilot suddenly became ill. With some assistance from the ailing pilot, I was able to make an emergency landing in Moncton, much to the relief of all on board, including myself.

Training Command did have its dangers. One of our aircraft got lost on a training flight, ran out of fuel, and landed on the ice in the Gulf of St. Lawrence. We were on the same exercise, and everybody operated on the same frequency. When I heard the SOS, I relayed the message to Charlottetown. Not all incidents had happy endings, however. Two of my fellow wireless operators are buried in Sherwood Cemetery as a result of flying accidents. Two others were lost when their planes were forced down in the Gulf of St. Lawrence, and their bodies were never recovered.

Training exercises during the Canadian winters were challenging. During the winter of 1941–42, when one of the windows in the Anson broke, I got frostbite on my face. One of the tricks we used to keep our feet warm was to thread wires through the soles of our flying boots and hook them into the battery of the radio. It worked like a charm.

I arrived in Charlottetown on December 29, 1940, and I met my future wife two days later on New Year's Eve. As I was standing outside a restaurant feeling very sorry for myself, a Canadian officer asked me if I had a light for his cigarette. Apparently, he was going to a house party, and he graciously asked me to come along. This act of hospitality changed the entire course of my life because I met the girl I would eventually marry at that party. We bumped into each other again later on, and the rest is history.

To make a long story short, our romance blossomed, and Bernice Wood and I were married. We enjoyed being together as a married couple until I was sent back to the U.K. in November 1943. We were permitted to stay in Canada for only three years, and my time was up. By that time, Bernice was expecting our first son who was born on D-Day, the following June.

After I returned to England, I was posted to a staging area at Devizes, east of Bath, where Princess Elizabeth, now Queen Elizabeth II, trained as a truck driver. When she was in camp, we ate very well, even having apple pie with cloves. After she left, it was back to Spam and boiled potatoes. Later, I was transferred to a station across from the Isle of Wight where I worked on a Forward Relay Station. The radar tracked our fighters out about seventy-two miles.

I was posted overseas once more, but this time it was to North Africa. First, we had an enjoyable stopover in Italy. This was 1944, and we were able to do some sightseeing in Rome and Naples since the Germans had left by that time. After a week and a half in Italy, we were flown to Cairo West Airport. There, I was the assistant in the Signals Section. After two or three weeks, I was posted to Khartoum. As the radio operator, I was part of a crew that was sent all over Africa, helping to transport personnel, freight and wild animals. The wild animals were caught by big game hunters, and we would take them to the zoo in Cairo.

VE Day was very memorable for me, but not in the usual sense. The crew and I were returning to Cairo when we had an engine failure, and we were forced to land in the desert. Unfortunately, we landed in soft sand. Because of the landing conditions, no plane could be sent to get us. During the four days we were there, we had only some chocolate bars, a couple of oranges and two cans of distilled water. On the second day there, we received a message informing us that the war was over, and there we were, stuck in the desert while everybody back at the base was whooping it up! Finally, sand tractors, a maintenance crew, a doctor, and another pilot reached us. The plane was repaired, dragged to a harder surface, and flown back to Khartoum.

Because I was part of the permanent forces, my number for demobilization did not come up until 1947, and then I returned to England. After I arrived, I made arrangements to leave the U.K. in order to be with my wife and son in Canada, but it took some time. I had enjoyed my time in Canada and wanted to spend the rest of my life there. When I left the U.K, my family was sad to see me go, and there were many tears at the dock in Liverpool when I boarded the *Mauritania*. It was not until 1948 that I was re-united with my wife, and I was able to see my son for the first time. He had been born four years earlier. I found a job at Maritime Electric working in the meter department. After about a year, I got a better job with the CNR doing electrical maintenance on diesel locomotives.

In my retirement years, I do volunteer work in the hospital. My other hobby is using my metal detector to find artifacts, a most enjoyable activity. To date, I have found lead balls from muskets, old broaches, pins, coins, ammunition and buttons at various places around the Island.

Unfortunately, my loving wife passed away in 1991. In June 2004, I married Muriel, a lovely lady who is the daughter of Charlie Chamberlain, the singer from the Don Messer Band. We both enjoy retirement in beautiful Prince Edward Island.

May 2006

ROBERT (BOB) W. METCALFE

OTTAWA, ONTARIO

Bob died on April 6, 2005, at the age of ninety. I was able to learn about his story from his wife, Helen, and from reading his book, No Time for Dreams: A Soldier's Six-Year Journey through WW II.

Bob was born in Richmond, North Yorkshire, on January 25, 1915. He graduated from Sandhurst Military Academy and enlisted in the 4th Battalion, The Green Howards, in December 1935. The Green Howards were part of the British Expeditionary Force that was sent to France in 1940 to help the French stop the advance of the German army. The campaign failed, and the Allies retreated to the port of Dunkirk on the northern coast of France to await transportation to Britain. Bob was wounded during this action. He was among the thousands of British and French soldiers who were transported safely across the Channel by the Royal Navy and hundreds of civilians in all manner of small craft.

After Bob recovered from his wounds in hospital, he rejoined his division, which had been posted to coastal defence in southern England. A German invasion was expected at any time. Hitler wanted to wipe out the RAF before he invaded England, and Bob witnessed many dogfights between the RAF and the Luftwaffe during the Battle of Britain. His unit lost six of their own because of a German air attack.

After the Germans invaded

Bob and Helen Metcalfe on their wedding day.
(Photo: Metcalfe Family)

Russia, the threat of a German invasion diminished, and the Green Howards, a rifle company, were posted to North Africa. They began their two-month journey on April 23, 1941. During part of the time, their convoy was shadowed by the German battleship, the *Bismarck*, but they did arrive safely in Port Tewfik, Suez, in early June 1941. The North African Campaign in the Western Desert, with Generals Montgomery and Rommel on centre stage, was underway.

The Green Howards spent two years in North Africa under abysmal conditions. They encountered extreme temperatures, awful food, water scarcity and, above all, sand, which found its way into everything. Thievery by the local people plagued the forces. Not content with taking the servicemen's possessions, marauding bands would steal the tents from over the heads of the sleeping soldiers who would wake up in astonishment the next morning under the hot sun. Many of these tents became the sails of the Arab falukas, flat-bottomed boats that plied the Nile.

The Allied Campaign in North Africa was successful. Thousands of German and Italian prisoners were taken, and General Rommel left for Germany in defeat. In June 1943, Bob was once again in a convoy, this time bound for Sicily. About this time, Bob was transferred from the Green Howards to a section of Eighth Army Headquarters. His new role was to help maintain supplies to the Eighth Army, a logistical challenge to say the least. When the Sicilian Campaign ended in success, the Allies crossed the Strait of Messina to begin the long, arduous journey through Italy.

While in Italy, Bob heard that a fuss was being made about the arrival of a certain Colonel Warden. He soon learned that this was the code name under which Winston Churchill travelled. While Churchill attended a meeting with senior officers, Bob was informed that an emergency had developed. Apparently, Churchill had run out of cigars! Bob came to the rescue, and was able to produce two boxes of White Owls for the colonel.

Bob recalled another amusing incident that occurred during his time in Italy. A funeral procession, with the usual solemnity, rituals, ecclesiastic robes, and funeral dirge, made its way down the Via Roma in Naples on the way to the cemetery. Two British intelligence officers, acting upon a tip, stopped the procession and removed the casket lid. The whole ceremony had been a sham. The coffin contained only olive oil that the perpetrators were going to dig up later that night to sell on the black market.

While Bob was stationed in Barletta, Italy, his commanding officer gave him a very important assignment. A Canadian hospital was being established in the area, and Bob was needed to entertain the nurses in the mess at HQ. He didn't know it at the time, but this assignment was to alter the course of his life. The nurses were from the No. 1 Canadian General Hospital and were part of the Royal Canadian Medical Corps. They had just arrived after experiencing a great deal of excitement during their voyage to Italy. One of the ships carrying some of the nurses had been sunk through enemy action, and although there was no loss of life, all personal belongings had been lost.

Bob arranged a reception for the nursing sisters which took place in a restaurant in Andria. The menu consisted of Asti Spumante [Italian champagne], octopus, local vegetables, and other rations from the mess at HQ. It was the first time that many soldiers had encountered English-speaking women since leaving Egypt, and the Canadian nursing sisters were very popular. Consequently, many friendships developed between the nursing sisters and the staff at HQ. According to Bob, the Canadian nursing sisters were more approachable and outgoing than the more reserved English nursing sisters in the area. Bob was smitten with Helen Porter, a physiotherapist attached to the Canadian hospital. Her duties included purchasing supplies for the sisters' mess.

Bob became a frequent visitor at the sisters' mess. Helen introduced Bob to a favourite drink that the nursing sisters called "steam." It was raw alcohol mixed with fruit juices. Although very pleasant to drink, steam had a delayed reaction with devastating results, as Bob discovered one Christmas Eve after an evening at the sisters' mess. On the way back to HQ, his jeep veered off the road and became stuck on a railway crossing. Bob couldn't go forward, couldn't go back and couldn't care less! From then on, he developed a new respect for the constitutions of the Canadian nurses. At this point, Bob had also come to the realization that he was in love.

Helen and Bob became engaged and tried to spend as much time together as possible. During their courtship, they explored historical and cultural sites in Rome and the surrounding areas. They even met the Pope at the Vatican. The local vineyards and hills were a perfect setting to celebrate their engagement, in spite of the war.

After Rome fell to the Allies, the Americans transferred several divisions to France to support the Normandy Invasion. This move caused a shortage of troops in the Fifth U.S. Army in Italy under General Mark Clark. Surplus British troops were transferred, and Bob was one of them. Although delighted with the largesse available in the American mess and the generosity of the American Red Cross, the move created a great distance between him and Helen, but they continued to correspond. Even though they were separated, they made arrangements for their wedding, which was to take place on October 28, 1944.

Since Mussolini had taken most of the gold to pay for the Abyssinian War, no wedding rings were available in Italy. Bob wrote to his parents in England and asked them to send a gold wedding ring and a diamond engagement ring through overseas mail, which was risky, since ships transporting mail could be sunk by U-boats or by the Luftwaffe. Fortunately, the parcel arrived three days prior to the wedding.

General Clark lent his jeep to Bob so that he and his best man could make the 200-mile journey to Jesi where Helen was stationed. According to Canadian law, unless you were Roman Catholic, all couples had to be married according to the laws of the country in which they were residing. Therefore, Bob and Helen had to be married by the mayor of Jesi. Conversely, according to British law, Bob had to be married by a British Army padre in order to receive an army marriage allowance. Bob and Helen were, therefore, married twice on the same day.

Because their marriage was the first one between Allied personnel in the city of Jesi, Bob and Helen's wedding ceremony was carried out with pomp and grandeur. The couple was escorted to the hall by two Italian *carabinieri* [policemen]. In the morning, the mayor conducted the service through an interpreter, kissed each of them on both cheeks, and gave Helen a bouquet of flowers.

At 3:00 p.m., a ceremony in the Anglican tradition was repeated by a British padre in the sisters' mess and was followed by a reception organized by Helen's roommates. With a container of cold chicken and a bottle of Scotch, a gift from the cook, the newlyweds set off on their honeymoon in General Clark's jeep. They spent the night in Perugia on the top floor of the Brufani Hotel.

The second night was spent in Florence in a suite at the British-requisitioned Savoy Hotel, which had been used the previous month by Goering. Bob's fellow officers arranged a reception for them, which General Clark and his staff attended. Florence was a very romantic place to spend a honeymoon, in spite of the fact that many of the famous works of art had been stolen by the Germans.

Canadian Army regulations stipulated that married couples could not reside in the same theatre of war for more than three months. Sadly, Helen returned to the U.K. in December and was assigned to No. 22 Canadian General Hospital at Horley in Sussex.

Eventually, the Italian Campaign wound down. Bob had been away from home for more than five years and was repatriated to the U.K. The war had sapped Britain's strength and, economically, conditions appeared bleak. Helen had to return to Canada to be demobilized, and there seemed few employment prospects for Bob in Britain. He learned that volunteers were required for a new battalion that would be stationed in Jamaica, and if he joined, Helen would be allowed to live there, too.

After the term in Jamaica ended, Bob and Helen returned to the U.K. in April 1947, and Bob was demobilized. Their daughter, Sharon, was born on September 16, 1947, and the family of three left for Canada on January 6, 1948. Thus, Robert W. Metcalfe became a war groom.

A second daughter, Susan, was born on May 4, 1952, and the family was complete. Bob became a Canadian citizen in 1955. Eventually, he and Helen were blessed with four grandchildren, their pride and joy. Bob was employed in Chatham, Ontario, as part of the sales staff of a wholesale hardware and steel company, retiring from this position in 1985.

Throughout his life in Canada, Bob did volunteer work and received many awards for services to his community. He was even nominated for the Order of Canada. In October 2004, Bob and Helen celebrated their sixtieth wedding anniversary.

Helen sent me a letter and asked that I include the following comments to my summary.

[When we arrived in Canada], we joined my parents in Windsor, Ontario. Here, Bob experienced all the advantages of Canada, and my family offered him a warm welcome. He was still a proud Englishman, a British "bride" groom, a Green Howard from Yorkshire and, as the story goes, a great new war groom welcomed by all Canadians. Bob's first encounter with Canada was awesome. He was a Brit, a husband, and a father in a completely different environment. Gone were the days of uncertainty, rationing, limited heat, and war-damaged buildings. Bob accepted the challenge of this new life and strove to make a new home for his family. I was also very happy to return to Canada.

Helen Metcalfe, December 2005

A. Edward (Eddie) Mills

CHARLOTTETOWN, PRINCE EDWARD ISLAND

I was born on July 14, 1917, at Wurthing, Sussex, England. I joined the RAF in 1940 and went to fight in France. I was injured during the Battle of Dunkirk and was sent home to recover. In 1941, when I was twenty-five years old, I was posted overseas to Charlottetown, Prince Edward Island. I was an aircraft technician, and it was my job to train other airmen in my field.

Whenever we were on leave, we usually went into town. One day in 1943, six other airmen and I met Jean and a group of her friends in Charlottetown. We started chatting as young people do, and Jean was the one who made the first move. She stole my hat and ran into Victoria Park where she finally let me catch up to her, and from that day, we have been inseparable.

We began to see each other regularly and, after a while, we became engaged. We were married on September 2, 1943, and because Jean was under twenty-one, she had to get her parents' permission. Her parents didn't want her to marry me and told her that she didn't know what my family was like. Jean's response was, "I'm not marrying his people; I'm marrying Eddie."

The war split us apart in 1944, and I had to return to England to continue to train airmen there until the end of the war. Jean, by that time, was expecting and wasn't very happy about having a child with no father about. I was heartbroken, of course, but I had to keep my mind on my job. We both carried on, and we couldn't let our minds wander. We wrote to each other every week, and I always referred to Jean in my letters as "My Little Chickadee."

Jean saved her money, and in June 1945, took our six-month-old baby to England in order to be with me. Jean travelled on the *Mauritania* with many other war brides who were eager to join their British husbands. The food on board was delicious and plentiful, and it would be a long time before Jean saw such meals again. She still has the ship's menu, complete with the signatures of the other war brides on the reverse side.

Jean and the baby stayed with my family at Wurthing and had to adjust to the rationing and the scarcity of food. I had to be away much of the time, but when we could be together, we shared what little food there was. Civilians were allowed one egg a week and a piece of meat the size of one's palm. Jean would stand in line at the butcher shop, and if she was lucky, she would get some bones to make a stew, a rare treat.

We stayed in England after the war, and I always told Jean that we could return to Prince Edward Island whenever she wanted. In all the time we were in England, there was only one incident that made Jean homesick. In 1946, we were lying on the bed listening to the radio when the announcer mentioned something that made her cry. He said, "Away down east

Eddie and Jean Mills shortly after they were married.
(Photo: Mills Family)

in Charlottetown, Prince Edward Island, here's Don Messer and the Islanders." Jean suddenly realized how much she missed home, and by December 1946, we were back on the Island where we have lived ever since.

I retired from the Agricultural Research Station in Charlottetown in 1982, and Jean has long since retired from her job as school secretary at West Kent School. We really enjoy retirement, and we have plenty of time to spend at our cottage at Nine-Mile Creek. We love to travel and have been to Florida, the Bahamas, Jamaica, Barbados, California, Arizona, and many parts of Canada. On our fifty-ninth anniversary, we took a second honeymoon by train to Niagara Falls. Our love affair, which began during the war, is still going on after sixty-two years, and it all began when Jean took my hat. I am very thankful that Jean made the first move.

January 2006

RONALD (RON) PARKINSON

WINNIPEG, MANITOBA

My husband, Ron Parkinson, was born in Astley, which is just outside of Manchester. He came to Canada to train as a bomb aimer in the summer of 1944 and was stationed in Dafoe, Saskatchewan. The big city of Winnipeg was a favourite destination for many airmen who trained in small communities such as Dafoe.

One time, Ron and his friend were in Winnipeg on leave when they happened to visit the T. Eaton Store on Portage Avenue. At that time, I worked at Eaton's, and one day when I was on my break, I went to the third floor to see my friend, Vera, who worked behind the meat counter. Love at first sight does occur, believe me, and Ron and I are a prime example of that old cliché. I spotted two airmen across the way, and the eyes of one of them looked into mine. Sparks flew! Rather flustered, I continued on. It so happened that the two airmen had walked the other way, and the four of us met at Vera's cash register. We starting chatting, and Vera, ever the organizer, made the arrangements for all four of us to go on a double date. Initially, Vera was paired off with Ron, but it soon became obvious to everyone that he and I were very attracted to each other. Thankfully, Vera was very understanding about it.

Ron and I started to see each other as often as we could, and we became serious very shortly. During our courtship, we often visited the Airmen's Club and The Cave in downtown Winnipeg. The Cave, a well-known nightclub, was a popular destination for young people, even though everyone had to sneak their liquor in and hide it under the table.

Before I met Ron, I had been dating Norman, a very nice airman in the RCAF who was taking his

Ron and Flo Parkinson shortly after they were married.
(Photo: Parkinson Family)

training at No. 3 Wireless School in Winnipeg. We saw each other frequently, but then he was posted somewhere in western Canada, and I didn't hear from him. Then I met Ron, and I forgot about Norm.

After I had been dating Ron for a while, I brought him home to meet my parents.

As I was introducing him to my parents, the phone rang. It was Norm calling from the train station. He was on his way to the war and had a short layover before he continued his journey to Halifax. He asked me if I would come to the train station to see him. There was no question about what I was going to do. I told Ron and my parents where I was going and why, and I left all three of them in wide-eyed bewilderment, an awkward situation to be sure. I met Norm at the train station and told him that although I liked him a lot, I had met someone whom I liked better. Norm was understanding and took the news better than I thought he would. Incidentally, Norm and I remain friends to this day, and we exchange Christmas cards each year. My parents came to love Ron almost as much as I did and were pleased with my choice, although they had liked Norm, too.

Our courtship was interrupted by a posting to Abbotsford, British Columbia. From there, Ron wrote a letter asking me to marry him, sending an engagement ring along with his proposal. I guess he remembered the incident with Norm, and he didn't want me to remain unattached too long. I don't know how our postman knew that there was a ring in the package, but he did. The ring cost about $40, quite a sum in those days. Ron's family in England was surprised at the news of our engagement, of course, and Aunt Agnes wrote a letter to her favourite nephew asking him to "think it over." Eventually, she and everyone else came around and accepted the fact that Ron was determined to marry a Canadian girl. In later years, I met Aunt Agnes, and she was wonderful to me. In fact, she left us a bit of money after she died.

Ron obtained permission from the RAF to get married. A naval chaplain married us on February 12, 1945, at Holy Trinity Anglican Church in Winnipeg. Unfortunately, I no longer have wedding pictures because they were destroyed in the infamous 1950 flood that inundated much of Winnipeg, including our home. Ron and I returned to Abbotsford after the wedding and began our married life in a rented room where we were blissfully happy. By the way, on our twenty-fifth anniversary, we renewed our vows at the same church where we were married.

All too soon, Ron was posted to India, even though the war was over by that time. When he left, I was pregnant with the first of our four children. Ron and his crew were kept busy dropping supplies and rice in the region. After a year in India, Ron returned to England, received his discharge papers, and made arrangements to come to Canada. Canada was the place where he wanted to spend the rest of his life. There was absolutely no question about it. He loved it here! We were eventually reunited, and our year-old daughter, Lynn, was introduced to her father for the first time. Later on, we had three more children—Ron, Kathy, and Rick.

Through friends, Ron got his first job in the City of Winnipeg Transit Building behind the Fort Garry Hotel doing electronic work. I now live in an apartment complex that was built on the site of that old transit building. Ron attended the University of Winnipeg during the evenings and received his degree in business. He was promoted and eventually worked in personnel and training for the City of Winnipeg.

Ron and I visited England on several occasions with our children, and we thoroughly enjoyed our visits. I particularly enjoyed the pubs and the old houses with the low beams. I still keep in touch with Ron's family, and my children have made many visits to see their relatives. In fact, my son is now living in London and absolutely loves it.

Ron was a school trustee for eighteen years, and we enjoyed going to school board conventions around the country. We had a good life, and we particularly loved camping with our children. Members of the British Wives Club often invited Ron and me to their functions, and those war brides know how to have a good time. I can't remember how many times we danced to "Knees Up, Mother Brown." Unfortunately, it was all over much too soon. Ron suffered a fatal heart attack in 1980 and died at the young age of fifty-seven.

I had a memorial plaque laid in the BCATP Garden of Memories at the 17th Wing at the airfield in Winnipeg. They hold a small ceremony there every September. The garden was made to remember the men who trained in Canada under the BCATP and who are now deceased.

Flo Parkinson, May 2006

STAN SMITH

BEAVERTON, ONTARIO

I was born in London, England. At the outbreak of war in 1939, I had just commenced my training as an accountant. After the evacuation of British and French forces at Dunkirk, I joined the Home Guard, ready to resist the anticipated invasion of the Germans. We trained with mock wooden rifles. Thank God there was no invasion! I observed the Battle of Britain by visiting relatives in Reigate, Surrey, in the south of England where I spent my visit lying on my back in the fields while the battle raged overhead. I observed the bombing of London from my home in a suburb. My grandparents' home was totally destroyed by a bomb. Fortunately, my grandparents were away at the time.

In February 1942, I enlisted in the Royal Air Force Volunteer Reserve for aircrew training and, after a time, graduated as a wireless operator / air gunner. My entire training took place in the United Kingdom. In November 1943, I was stationed at No. 6 Advanced Flying Unit in preparation for a final posting to an operational training unit and, from there, to a bomber command squadron. There were thirty WOP/AGs in my unit. Several days before the completion of our training, we received a request for twelve volunteers for overseas service. The location was secret, of course, but we all thought it was the Middle East. Thirty hands shot into the air, although only twelve were needed. Thirty scraps of paper were provided, and twelve were marked with an "X". The papers were put into a hat, and we each drew one. I was lucky. It was one of the few times that I have been successful in a draw, but this one altered my entire life.

After embarkation leave, we reported to the depot for overseas equipment, and we still did not know where we were going. After we boarded the *Aquitania*, we were advised that we could write home and could give our forwarding address as "RCAF, Ottawa, Canada." Never in our wildest dreams had we expected to be posted to Canada! We had done our entire training in the U.K. Why Canada? That question was answered by several returning airmen from Ferry Command.

After five days at sea, submarine alerts, and very rough weather, we arrived at New York. After three years of blackouts, the bright lights of the city were a wonderful

Stan and Ruth Smith on their wedding day.
(Photo: Smith Family)

sight. We boarded a train for Montreal and had our first Canadian meal in the dining car. What a feast! The food and service were superb.

Upon arrival in Montreal in February 1944, we were taken to Doval Airport which, at that time, was on the outskirts of the city. We were now part of No. 45 Group Atlantic Transport Command. Our job was to deliver to the U.K. and the Middle East lend-lease aircraft supplied by the United States.

RAF Ferry Command was formed in July 1941. It was a unique organization in those years. It employed many civilians: pilots, radio officers, mechanics, maintenance people, cleaners, cafeteria workers, etc. The Command built the large airport at Dorval with a training base, No. 313 Ferry Training Unit, at North Bay, Ontario. RAF Ferry Command became No. 45 Group Atlantic Transport Command in March 1943. The slow replacement of civilian flying personnel with service personnel began, and we were part of that replacement.

In April of 1944, our group of twelve was sent to North Bay for a six-week training course, and this is where I first met Ruth Elizabeth Norman. Neither Dorval nor North Bay had messing facilities for service personnel. The Command was operating cafeterias at both locations, and these supplied the wants of the civilians. In lieu of service facilities, we were paid a messing allowance, and we ate all our meals at the cafeterias. Ruth was a cashier at the North Bay cafeteria. My first encounter with her was when I bought my first meal upon arrival. We eventually dated, and as we both loved to dance, we attended many functions during my six-week stay. At the end of the six weeks, our group returned to Dorval to begin the delivery work that we had been sent over to do.

None of us expected to see North Bay again, and we had said tearful good-byes to the many young ladies we had met and socialized with during our stay. From May until October 1944, we made deliveries to both the U.K. and the Middle East. Imagine my surprise when I was informed in late October that I was to be returned to North Bay as part of the regular training staff. (I was there until November 1945.) Imagine Ruth's surprise when I returned! Three meals a day brought me face to face with Ruth at her cash register. The friendship developed into a romance, an engagement, and a marriage in November 1945. Shortly thereafter, the decision was made to close the base at North Bay, and I was ordered back to the U.K.

In December 1945, I returned to the U.K. aboard the SS *Mauretania*, sailing from Halifax. In February 1946, the RAF provided passage for Ruth aboard the SS *Lochmonar*, a freighter with accommodation for fifty passengers, twelve of whom were war brides. Ruth arrived in the U.K. in the midst of the worst winter in many years. There were shortages of everything: housing, food, heat, clothing, you name it! Upon my release from the RAF in November 1946, I resumed my accounting studies. During this time, we were living with my parents. Ruth took a part-time position with a hostel management group to add to our income. We decided to emigrate, and at that time, Australia had a very aggressive immigration program. For a minimal cost, the Australian government would provide all the necessary support for new immigrants, and Ruth and I were impressed. Ruth, being Canadian, however, preferred to return to her roots. We agreed to register our names with both the Australian and Canadian authorities, and we would take the first one that could arrange passage for us. Canada won!

After my discharge from the RAF, we returned to Canada in June 1947 aboard the MV *Marine Falcon*. This vessel was a converted American troopship, and there were many American war brides on board. The ladies had cabin accommodation, and the men had dormitory berths. It was an interesting trip. We arrived back in North Bay in July 1947. In November 1947, we moved to Sudbury, Ontario, which was our home until 1995. Then, we moved to Beaverton, Ontario, to be closer to our daughter, son and family. During our stay in Sudbury, we were both active in community and public affairs. I joined the RCAF Supplementary Reserve and became second-in-command of the local air cadet unit, an enjoyable experience.

Ruth and I have had, and are still having, a wonderful marriage. We have been married over sixty years. We are suffering from the usual old age ailments. The mild stroke Ruth had four years ago restricts her activities, but she maintains a wonderful outlook on life. We used to travel to the U.K. once every five years to visit my family, but the last trip was in 1996. My sister passed away in December 2005. She was the last surviving family member. We no longer have any ties with that country.

The Smiths are now fully Canadian.

Several of my RAF colleagues also married Canadian girls when they were stationed in Canada during the war. We thought that as the Canadian servicemen in the U.K. were stealing our girls, we should steal a few of theirs to try to even matters.

June 2006

ARTHUR (ART) STEBBING

PENTICTON, BRITISH COLUMBIA

*Art and Marjorie Stebbing
on their wedding day.*
(Photo: Stebbing Family)

I was born in London, England, on October 25, 1921, and I joined the Royal Navy in January 1941. Little did I know at the time that I would eventually go to Canada.

At first, I was with the convoys near the U.K., mostly in the North Sea and the Irish Sea. In 1942, I was on an "ack-ack" ship called HMS *Alynbank*, escorting convoys from Iceland to Russia. I made two trips in that ship to Archangel, and we were heavily bombed by the Germans who were based in Norway. We lost seven ships on the first convoy and thirteen on the second. When I returned to England, I took part in the invasion of North Africa in November 1942 [Operation Torch]. We took the convoy from England and Scotland through the Bay of Biscay and the Mediterranean to Oran, staying there until Christmas 1942.

When we returned to our base in Scotland, I was posted to Portsmouth where I took a course for leading seaman and qualified for a higher gunner rate. I was then posted to an aircraft carrier called the HMS *Ameer*, and I served on that ship until the end of the war. It was commissioned in October 1943 in Vancouver where I met my future wife, Marjorie McRae.

The carrier had been built in the States, but had been sent to Vancouver to have the guns put on it, and we were to pick it up there. In November 1943, four girls were walking down Granville Street, and four sailors were walking up the street. We turned round, and the girls turned round. We learned that they were going to a show, and we asked if we could join them. We went to the show, and when we came out,

*Art and Marjorie Stebbing
on their wedding day.*
(Photo: Stebbing Family)

Marjorie phoned her mother to ask if she could bring four sailors home. At the time, she was sixteen, and the other girls were also under age. That was the stipulation imposed upon them. If they met any servicemen, they were to bring them home. If the servicemen wouldn't come home, they were to leave them where they found them.

In walked four sailors and four girls, but Marjorie's mother was unfazed. She put the kettle on and proceeded to feed us. I learned later that we were the first servicemen the girls had met, and they were very excited. Marjorie's mother put us up for the night, got us up the next morning, made us breakfast, and got us to the streetcar so we could get back to the ship. We visited Marjorie's home two more times before we left Vancouver. On one of those occasions, Marjorie's mom made a beautiful dinner for us. She invited a couple of war orphans who lived on the street and some neighbours.

Even though we had only seen each other three times, the girls promised to write to us, but Marjorie and I were the only ones who stuck with it. We wrote to each other for just over two years and got to know each other that way. We learned a lot about each other and discovered that we thought alike on many matters. The fact that Marjorie had beautiful red hair and a nice figure was an added bonus. In time, I sent Marjorie an engagement ring from South Africa. In our letters, we discussed marriage, but it seemed impossible under the circumstances.

Meanwhile, the war continued. After I returned to Scotland, I completed my training, and I served in the Far East on the HMS *Ameer* from the spring of 1944 until hostilities against the Japanese ceased in August 1945. We were in the Bay of Bengal for the next eighteen months, based in Trincomalee, now Sri Lanka. Our task was to carry out air strikes against Japanese airfields in order to prevent the enemy from supporting their ground troops fighting in Burma. On one occasion, we were attacked by a Kamikaze dive-bomber but, fortunately for us, we shot him down before he could crash into our flight deck.

Most of our patrols were uneventful, as the war was winding down. The Japanese were concentrating on the defence of their bases in the Pacific, and our theatre of war in the Bay of Bengal was drawing to a close. We encountered little resistance in the closing months of the war. Our final task was to drop supplies to our ailing prisoners of war at Kuala Lumpur.

The HMS *Ameer* was a lend-lease ship from the U.S., and it had to be returned after the war. We returned the carrier, along with 400 American servicemen, to Norfolk, Virginia. From there, I was granted permission to go to Vancouver, and I phoned Marjorie's mother to tell her I was coming. I told her that Marjorie and I were going to talk to see if we really wanted to get married. As it happened, her mother was hard of hearing, and misunderstood me. She thought that I said that I was coming to Vancouver to marry Marjorie. Her mother rushed around, got the church booked, got our marriage license, and arranged everything else. I arrived in Vancouver by train on January 16, 1946, and three days later, on the 19th, I was married. An old boyfriend of Marjorie's was my best man, and her brother gave her away. The night before we got married, I asked Marjorie if she really wanted to go through with it. She said, "I will if you do," and so we really started out as strangers. All of her friends said it would never last, but sixty years later, we are still going strong. Years later, Marjorie told me that she was attracted to me because of my smile and blue eyes.

I never went back to England, and I was able to get demobilized in Esquimalt on Vancouver Island. After my release, I had a few jobs, and finally ended up with *The Province* [newspaper] as a proofreader. I really enjoyed that job, but the timing was bad, and there was a strike. I decided to go back into the Service, but Marjorie didn't want me to go into the navy because that meant I would be away from home a lot. I had been a member of the Auxiliary Air Force, and because I really enjoyed it, I decided to join the RCAF in January 1950. I never regretted this decision, and we had some wonderful years.

Right after I joined, I had to go east for training, and it was six months before Marjorie and the boys could join me. Our first son had been born in January 1947, and the second in June 1949. We had two years in Trenton, and then we were transferred to England where we stayed for three years. My parents were delighted with this posting because they got a chance to see their grandsons. Throughout the years I was in the Service, we've lived at various places. We've been stationed in Toronto, Vancouver, Winnipeg (twice), France (five years), Germany (five years), and then we came to Penticton in 1973, where we have been ever since. It has been a wonderful life, and we wouldn't change a bit of it for anything.

The Service has been good to us. When we were posted in France and Germany, we were able to tour Europe. We could visit another country on a Sunday afternoon, and we never would have had that opportunity if I hadn't been in the Service. We never owned our own home until we came to Penticton. It is paradise here. Until I developed Parkinson's disease, I was healthy, energetic, and game for anything. Marjorie says that I was best the dancer at the mess dances. She was always complaining that all the other wives wanted to dance with me, and that she hardly got a chance. We started out with nothing, and we stuck it out through thick and thin. We celebrated our sixtieth anniversary last January.

May 2006

C. Richard Taylor

WILLIAMS LAKE, BRITISH COLUMBIA

I was born in Hucknall, Nottinghamshire, on November 20, 1923. I enjoyed a happy family childhood with two younger brothers and caring parents. I joined the RAF on my eighteen birthday in 1941.

I completed initial training and flying grading school in England and flew solo after ten hours of instruction. I came to Canada with the BCATP and completed elementary and service flying training in Alberta before being posted to Flying Instructors' School in Arnprior, Ontario, in November 1943. During the last phase of my training, I met Corporal Muriel A. Herbert, RCAF, Women's Division (Statistics Department).

Muriel was born in Vancouver on May 18, 1923, and joined the RCAF in November 1942. After basic training, she had various

Richard and Muriel Taylor during their courtship.
(Photo: Taylor Family)

postings and was eventually sent to No. 3 Flying Instructors' School in Arnprior where I was. As each new course arrived, the girls would pick the name of a pilot and have lots of bets to see if they could get to date him. She picked me, Dickie Taylor, as I was known then.

After I was posted to Arnprior, I soon learned that social life was an important factor on the station. All personnel were very friendly, particularly the non-commissioned ranks. However, that was not a problem when it came to doing our jobs. There was always some nightly entertainment, be it a film or a dance, or just a happy evening in the canteen or mess. There were four messes: airmen's, corporals', sergeants' and officers'. There was also a large hall which was a common social centre.

Richard and Muriel Taylor in uniform.
(Photo: Taylor Family)

Just down the road from the camp was a dance hall that was used by many of the service people. I remember being there with a friend on the same course as myself, and we were eyeing a couple of WDs [Women's Division, RCAF]. We decided to ask them to dance, and I happened to pick on Muriel Herbert. We danced and enjoyed the evening. I cannot remember too many of the earlier details, but I do remember taking one WD to the show one night, and then taking Muriel to the dance afterwards. Muriel and I just seemed to get together and kept seeing each other. I remember when she had the flu. I visited her in hospital and thought how nice she looked in pyjamas. She went away for Christmas to a friend's home, and I guess I was lonely while she was away. We had talked a lot and really enjoyed each other's company.

New Year's came and Muriel was invited to the dance in the sergeants' mess, just as I was. That was the first time I saw her in a dress. After midnight and "Auld Lang Syne," we went outside where a few visitors' cars were parked and, finding one unlocked, we got in the back seat. There, I asked her to marry me. She said, "Yes."

The next day, we went to Montreal on leave for a few days with another couple and had a happy time together. I was later posted to Moncton to prepare for my return to England, but as time dragged on, I got leave, and we were married on February 22, 1944. We had a brief honeymoon in Ottawa before I was sent back to England six weeks after our wedding.

It was a fast courtship and, of course, a lot of wartime marriages went sour. The fact that we had similar upbringings and both came from Christian families created a very strong bond between us. A commitment had been made, and we were both determined to keep it. We had promised to remain together "as long as we shall live." After sixty-two years, we are still together.

Muriel's parents had no objection to our engagement and readily gave their consent. As far as I was concerned, however, I only had to get permission from my CO. After we were married in Canada, I had sent a telegram to my family in England. Needless to say, the news of our marriage was a shock to my family. There was some concern later on when my family learned that Muriel was Catholic. I was brought up in a Baptist family. Muriel found an ally in my mother, who let it be known to all and sundry that there would be no interference with her beliefs, and things went well from then on.

After I returned to England, I was sent on several courses. After the disastrous airborne assault on Arnhem during which many glider pilots were lost, a good number of RAF pilots were transferred to the 6th Airborne Glider Pilot Regiment. After some fairly intense commando training, I became one of the pilots who flew a glider over the Rhine to secure a foothold for the advancing armies. Later, I was transferred back to the RAF and was demobilized in 1946.

During this time, Muriel was posted to Ottawa, and after applying for a discharge, returned to Vancouver. She was able to get passage to England sponsored by the RAF. The Atlantic crossing was frightening, and the convoy she was in got attacked one night during a storm. During the attack, a bunk bed tipped over on Muriel's leg, but she eventually landed safely in England and met my family for the first time.

After my discharge from the RAF, we settled in Hucknall, my hometown, and rented a house from my father, who worked in the clothing industry making Shetland shawls on very ancient hand frames. We tried to bring Muriel's parents over to England for a holiday, but after endless efforts, we always came up against a brick wall due to monetary exchange problems. Therefore, Muriel asked my father if we could go to Canada instead, and he agreed, with the provision that we return to England. We spent four very happy months in Canada, and this was the first time I had met Muriel's family. We had two children by that time, and another was born when we returned from the Canadian trip.

In 1952, we decided to return to Canada for good, and we left England in April 1953. Because Muriel was a returning veteran, we were fortunate to get our first house from Central Mortgage and Housing, and we joined a multitude of other veterans and their families living in Fraserview in South Vancouver. I do lay claim to being the only war groom in that area. These houses were rentals, but we were able to buy them after a few years, which we did. We finally sold the vet's house and moved to Richmond.

I had joined Jantzen Canada Inc. in the swimwear and sportswear industry a year after arriving in Canada and spent twenty-eight years with the company. Our family increased to a total of nine over the next few years and, of course, Muriel had her hands full during this time. After our last daughter was born, Muriel was in hospital with a very troublesome ulcer which had to be operated on.

Soon after she was back on her feet, Muriel began to get interested in childminding, and we started seeing babies and toddlers around the house. We became very attached to two boys in particular and, of course, their parents. Friendships are still ongoing to this day. Muriel decided to take courses in pre-school supervising, and after our youngest went to school, she became involved with a pre-school in Richmond and actually had some of our grandchildren in her classes.

In 1981, we left Richmond and started a new life in Williams Lake, B.C., on the advice of the parents of one of Muriel's long-term boys who had moved there. We ran a small store selling sewing machines and doing clothing alterations. Muriel worked at this for a while, but continued with her pre-school studies. Eventually, she and another lady were instrumental in opening the Sacred Heart Pre-school. She graduated as a pre-school supervisor and was with the school until we retired. We sold the store and our house in 1989 and went to live in Revelstoke and, later, Salmon Arm. We finally returned to Williams Lake in 2003. Our two youngest children are there with their families.

We have nine children, all living in B.C. There are twenty-three grandchildren and six great-grandchildren, with another one expected in August. Muriel and I have been truly fortunate.

April 2006

FREDERICK (FRED) TAYLOR

STRATFORD, ONTARIO

I was born in 1919 at South Shields in the County of Durham. My father was a police officer, and we lived in apartments within the police station. I enlisted in the RAF on March 28, 1939, six months before the outbreak of the war and, after basic training, was assigned to the Accountant Branch to serve at RAF Station Drem, East Lothian, Scotland. Drem was a Fighter Command station housing Spitfire and Hurricane aircraft.

I was supposed to be a groomsman at my sister's wedding on November 27, 1940, but the RAF had other plans for me. I left that day from Glasgow bound for Canada as part of the first draft of 500 airmen who were to become the operational staff at No. 33 Service Flying Training School at Carberry, Manitoba. Eventually, the station strength would number 1,500. I came over on the French liner, the *Louis Pasteur*, which had been seized in Marseilles by the British when France capitulated to the Germans. Unfortunately, the British did not have access to the specifications. Engine failure was experienced about two days after leaving Glasgow, and the ship came to a complete stop for about four hours. This was a dangerous situation in U-boat-patrolled waters, as we were unescorted. However, the day was saved when a British Coastal Command Flying Boat came to our rescue and dropped depth charges not far from us.

Fred and Charlotte Taylor on their wedding day.
(Photo: Taylor Family)

We arrived in Halifax and boarded the train, from which we had our first view of the Canadian countryside, which held many of us spellbound by its beauty and immense size. We reached Carberry on the evening of December 8, 1940, in the midst of a prairie winter.

My assignment at the station was to look after all the accounting relating to contracted supplies and labour and to recommend payment. The contract charges for the initial building of the base at Carberry were about $1 million, a substantial sum in those days. The base really stimulated the local economy, which had been hard hit by the Depression of the thirties. Merchants in the construction industry did particularly well, and the whole area began to thrive.

On the day of our arrival in Carberry, my wife-to-be, Charlotte Dennstedt, was in church sitting in the choir loft. The whole town knew about the arrival of the British airmen, and Charlotte admitted that, during the service, she was so excited that she could not pay attention to the sermon. After church, the girls went "downtown," and there were airmen everywhere! Some months were to pass before I eventually met Charlotte. In the meanwhile, we were indeed impressed by the kindness and hospitality of the local people.

I met Charlotte at a dance in town. I asked her to dance and said, "I'm not a very good dancer." Charlotte disagreed saying that I was pretty good. She was a farm girl from Fairview, Manitoba. We met several times in town, and I often walked out to the farm. On one of these occasions, I suffered multiple mosquito bites. The facial swelling distorted my features to the extent that Charlotte barely recognized me.

During our life together, we have often looked back at the time when we individually realized that marriage was looking like a possibility. Charlotte has referred many times to the occasion when she prepared a dinner for two composed of sautéed prairie chicken and all the trimmings. She thought that the way to an Englishman's heart was through his stomach. Jokingly, she often has told me that this was the time she felt that she had me hooked. I told her just recently that while I appreciated all her efforts with the prairie-chicken thing, it was not the precise moment of the important decision. It was more of an accumulation of things ending with us both seated at the organ. Charlotte was singing in the most beautiful soprano voice with such sincerity. I was completely overwhelmed. Such a delightful voice! This event proved to be the clincher, and I wanted to spend the rest of my life with her.

After our sojourn at the organ, we went into the kitchen, and it was there I proposed. However, being rather old-fashioned by Canadian standards, I insisted upon having her parents' sanction and blessing. I left Charlotte in the kitchen while I entered their living room to discuss the matter with her parents. They readily granted their permission. Charlotte told me afterwards that she had her ear glued to the kitchen door, and was ready to embrace me as I re-entered the kitchen.

We were married on July 24, 1943, in Knox Presbyterian Church. Charlotte's matron of honour was her older sister, Mary, and the soloist was her sister, Letha, singing "Oh Perfect Love." My best man was my friend, Flight Sergeant Arthur Gooderich. The wedding reception was held on the farm lawn. Preceding the reception, we had a flypast when two planes from the base flew low over the lawn. We spent our honeymoon in Brandon and at Clear Lake in Riding Mountain National Park. There, we rented a boat, did a little swimming, and got sunburned to boot, which had the effect of cooling down our honeymoon for a day or two.

We were together from July to November 1943, when I was sent back to Britain. Charlotte was given permission to go to Britain, but had to wait about nine months until a passage was available. While she waited, she stayed with her oldest sister in Pickering, Ontario, where she got a job in a munitions plant. She left for Britain with other war brides on our first wedding anniversary. Charlotte said that when her parents saw her off, they looked like they were at a funeral. They did not expect to see her again.

I was posted to No. 73 Wing at No. 12 Group Headquarters at Malton, Yorkshire, and then was farmed out to one of their radar stations situated at Cleadon, which was right in my hometown at South Shields.

I had been told of Charlotte's impending arrival, but for the sake of security, no dates were given, nor was I informed she was crossing the Atlantic by convoy. There was no indication of the port of arrival, and I was not allowed to meet her. She had to travel from the port of disembarkation to my hometown with directions. When she finally arrived, she was to meet all her new relatives for the first time. What a day!

Early in 1945, I was posted to RAF Station Bodorgan, situated on the Isle of Anglesey, just off the coast of Wales. Since this station was also a holding unit for Italian prisoners of war, I was sent on a prisoner-of-war course. When I completed the course, I was to attend to the prisoners' needs and settle any conflicts, in addition to my accounting responsibilities. I think the Italians were glad to be prisoners and out of the war.

It was at this station when I was recommended for a commission. I suggested that I would be interested in the Equipment Branch rather than the Accountant Branch. Shortly after, I was told that I was being posted to South East Asia Command, and that I was to take fourteen days' embarkation leave. I immediately thought of Charlotte. It occurred to me that I might just as well have left her in Canada instead of dumping her down in a country of strangers. The senior accountant officer told me that he would try to arrange an interview for me with the Officer Selection Board at the Air Ministry in London before the embarkation date. Three days later, I received a telegram indicating that I was to be interviewed in London in two days. In many ways, my future depended on the success of this interview. Remuneration in the RAF was much lower than equivalent ranks in the RCAF, and there was no opportunity to accumulate savings required to return to Canada.

When I boarded the overnight train to London, I was thoroughly groomed: my brass buttons were dazzling, and the seams in my slacks were razor sharp. The carriage had seats on either side with a corridor up the middle. The train stopped at Darlington to pick up passengers who had to stand up in the aisle because all the seats were occupied. One of these passengers had consumed far too much alcohol and expelled the excess by vomiting over me from head to foot. I had to suffer the odour all the way to London, and it was obvious that I could not present myself for an interview in that state at 10:00 a.m. I noticed a Salvation Army outlet, and I explained my predicament to the lady behind the counter. She took me to a room, gave me a blanket, and told me she would be back in five minutes to pick up my clothes for cleaning. I don't know how she did it so early in the morning but, shortly, everything was back on track, and I left with a renewed spring in my step. Since that day, I have a soft spot in my heart for the Salvation Army, which because of this act of kindness was instrumental in my return to Canada. A day or two later, I received a telegram advising me to return to my unit as my overseas posting had been cancelled.

After completing training at Officer Cadet College, I was posted to Fighter Command Headquarters for redirection to RAF Station Acklington, Northumberland, where I served as the equipment officer. I also served at Barton Hall at the RAF Observer School, as well as being commanding officer of an adjacent Italian prisoner-of-war camp. From there, I was posted to Linton-on-Ouse in Yorkshire, where I served as the equipment officer. I ended my service returning to RAF Station Acklington, where I served as the senior equipment officer.

I was released from the RAF on March 28, 1948. I sailed for Canada on April 1, 1948, with my wife and fifteen-month-old daughter, Marguerite. At the beginning of July, I was hired as the purchasing agent for the town of Dryden in Ontario. In 1951, I was offered the job as hospital administrator there.

After the building and furnishing of a new hospital in Dryden, I was offered a job as the administrator of a new hospital to be built in Manitouwadge in northern Ontario. I accepted the position, remaining there twelve years. When the job as director of finance opened up at a hospital in Stratford, I applied and got the job. I

On leave in Carberry, Manitoba. Airmen from
No. 33 SFTS enjoy the hospitality of a local family.
(Photo: Carberry Plains Archives)

retired from this job twenty-two years ago.

Charlotte and I have a daughter and a son. We have three grandchildren, one great-grandson and twin great-grandchildren on the way. I have no regrets about coming to Canada. It was one of the best decisions I ever made. We still live in Stratford and enjoy it very much. Our last visit to Britain was in 1996, and I only have one sister left there.

Charlotte's sight has diminished to the extent that she can no longer read or distinguish colours, and we do the shopping together. She does, however, look as beautiful as ever, and total strangers, while shopping, have commented to us how well we look together. After sixty-two years of marriage, the wedding solo was most appropriate—"Oh Perfect Love."

On looking back upon my nine years with the RAF, I realize that it was a period of excitement, comradeship, and diligence in the performance of one's duties. I remember the last day of my service, and I was free to go home the next day. However, the next day, I felt obligated to go on parade for the last time, and with a lump in my throat, I said my good-byes and wondered what the future held in store for me. The thought of being with my wife, Charlotte, every day for the rest of my life was to be a new and comforting experience.

October 2005

IVOR WILLIAM (BILL) THOMAS

WINNIPEG, MANITOBA

Bill was my stepfather-in-law. After he died on February 25, 2005, the family found his brief memoirs among his papers. Because Bill's wartime marriage didn't survive the stresses of civilian life, he failed to give any details about this relationship in his memoirs. Not all hasty wartime marriages had fairytale endings.

In order for the reader to understand Bill's story, it is necessary to provide some background information. When the airmen from No. 33 SFTS in Carberry came to Winnipeg on leave, billets would be found for them. On one of his leaves, Bill stayed at the home of a Winnipeg couple who had a daughter. They began to see each other whenever Bill came to Winnipeg. The relationship became serious, and they were married just before Bill was sent overseas to serve with Bomber Command. After the war, Bill returned to Canada. The marriage, which produced two sons and two daughters, ended in divorce in 1966. I don't know the reasons for the failure of the marriage, but Bill's job with the CNR, which took him away from his family for much of the time, had to have been one of the factors. At the time of this writing, Bill's ex-wife was still living.

An excerpt from Bill's memoirs:

I was born on January 1, 1921, in the upstairs bedroom of 19 Powell Street, Old Trafford, Manchester, England. We were a medium-poor, low-middle class, Welsh family. After I finished school, I got a job as apprentice draftsman with Edward Wood Steel Fabricators. I attended Engineering Night School at Salford Tech and took courses at Manchester University. My dad, who was a semi-pro musician, taught me to play the string bass, and I got a permanent job playing in a dance band on Friday and Saturday nights.

We lived close to Old Trafford, the home of Manchester United Football Club. On Saturday afternoons, Dad and I would join 50,000 other fans to watch the game. There were no seats, and everybody stood on terraced steps, "belly-to-bum," as it was commonly termed. Vigilance was necessary, because sometimes men would relieve themselves in the pockets of those standing in the row ahead. True, believe me!

War was declared in 1939, and my dad became the air-raid warden for our street.

There was a big flap about spies, saboteurs, etc., and the Home Guard was formed. They were issued ancient rifles without bullets and had to stand guard at their workplaces for one full night per week, hoping to God that no one showed up. I spent time with the Home Guard until I joined up, and I didn't mind at all. I was taught many previously unknown facts of life as well as cribbage and blackjack poker. The rotten breakfasts dished up by the cook prepared me for the Service and for prisoner-of-war camp.

Bill and Dorothy Thomas shortly after they were married.
(Photo: Kozar Family)

In early 1940, I took off for the RAF. I signed on as an AC2, a rank slightly lower than a snake's belly. I experienced one painful month of square-bashing and bullshit [drill / basic training] in the beautiful seaside resort of Paignton in Devon. Then, I was assigned to RAF Station Booker, near High Wycombe, where I learned to fly the Tiger Moth, an old single-engine biplane. I enjoyed this aircraft more than any other that I flew later. For the two months I spent there, I was in another world.

On graduation day in December 1941, I was promoted from AC2 to LAC, and was permitted to wear the white flash on my cap. We then proceeded to Glasgow, where we boarded a Norwegian cattle boat, the SS *Bergensfjord* and sailed for Canada. We were in a convoy comprised of three small ships escorted by three Royal Navy corvettes, and the going was rough. I was fortunate, or unfortunate, depending on how one looks at it, to have a strong stomach. As a result of my strong constitution, I spent New Year's Day 1942, my twenty-first birthday, on deck emptying puke buckets over the side of the ship. It took twelve long days to cross the Atlantic.

We arrived in Halifax on January 10, 1942, and boarded the CPR train for points west. I was dropped off at Carberry, Manitoba, along with about fifteen others. There, we learned to fly the Avro Anson.[10]

Upon graduation, four of us received commissions as pilot officers. We had a week's leave, and my buddy and I went to Niagara Falls and St. Catharines, Ontario, where I visited my mom's distant cousin. We then went to Moncton, bound for the U.K., but because a bottleneck had formed and no ships were available for us, our entire course was shipped back to airfields across Canada. I ended up in Calgary. Later, I was sent to New York where I joined about 10,000 American troops on board the *Queen Mary*. Without escort, we arrived in Greenock, Scotland, less than four days later.

There, I was posted to Grantham RAF Station, where we flew Oxfords at night to get us used to blackout conditions. Then, we were off to RAF Cottesmore, an operational training unit, where we learned to fly Vickers Wellingtons. Next, we went to RAF Scampton, where I met up with my crew. At first, we flew Avro Manchesters, twin-engined heavy bombers. On our first trip as a crew, our port engine blew up. It flew like a cow on one engine, but to the relief of my crew, I managed to land it safely. We later converted to the Avro Lancaster, the best bomber of the war.

We operated out of a mudhole called RAF Bardney, Lincolnshire. All went reasonably well until the night of May 22, 1943, when we set off to bomb Dortmund in the Rühr. After we dropped our bombs, we turned to go home, but we were coned [illuminated by searchlights], and almost immediately hit by a flak shell in the rear of the aircraft. The next thing I knew, we were in a steep dive. The gyro-compass had upset, and none of the instruments seemed to work. I had to ask Scottie [a crew member, likely the flight engineer] to help me haul back on the control column, and we managed to pull out at about 3,000 feet. By this time, we were over Essen, and it seemed that all the flak in the Third Reich opened up on us. Very shortly, both engines were on fire. As I tried to feather the engines and to start the fire extinguishers, there were more hits on the fuselage, and hydraulic fluid and

---

[10] A few years ago, when we were passing Carberry on the Trans-Canada Highway in order to attend a family wedding in Calgary, Bill pointed out the exact field where he and his instructor made an emergency landing.

oil was sprayed all over us. I gave the order, "Abandon aircraft!" As I tried to hold the aircraft more or less upright, my crew brushed past to dive out the hatch. I could not raise anyone else on the intercom, or see anybody left on the plane. I put on my chest chute and dived out.

I pulled the ring immediately, and I was soon hanging from a tree, twenty feet above ground, half strangled and dazed. Later, I remembered that I had forgotten to take off my helmet, and the intercom cable had been caught up by the chute shrouds. It's a wonder that my head didn't come off. I then punched the chute release and dropped down on the ground to face a pistol in the hands of a very large *Feldspolitzel* [German policeman]. I did not give him any argument at all!

I spent the night in the slammer at Essen, and the next day, I was taken to the infamous Luftwaffe interrogation centre in Frankfurt, where I spent several unpleasant days. Afterwards, I was taken to the main POW camp for air force crews, Stalag Luft 3 at Sagan, where there were several hundred Allied airmen.[11]

The camp had been operating about two years and was well established and supplied by the Red Cross. There was a band operating in camp, and as they had a bass fiddle and no one to play it, I joined in. Because of my previous dance band experience, I was asked to take over the band. I taught my friend, Mike, how to play the bass fiddle, while I made horrible noises on the trombone as I proceeded to learn its intricacies. We used to give concerts for the camp, and even the German officers used to come.

About January 1945, we were told to get our gear together, and we were marched out of camp, headed west on a four- or five-day march. The Russians were coming. We ended up at a place called Luckenwalde, about thirty miles south of Berlin. It was a rotten place, but we were better off than the Russian prisoners who had been there for a long time. About the end of April, we woke up to find that the German guards had left. We knew why when we witnessed the arrival of a Russian tank column. We were told by the Russians to stay put, "for documentation." Mike and I didn't care for the sound of that. We disobeyed orders, sneaked out the back door, and hitched a ride with the Russian tank column.

As it turned out, we saved ourselves a long, tedious journey home, although I now realize that we took a somewhat dumb chance. But Welsh spirits, or someone else, looked after us. "On to Berlin!" the tankers said, plying us with vodka which tasted like gasoline. Because we had not eaten for a while, we were soon very drunk and

---

[11] This camp was the scene of The Great Escape, which Paul Brickhill described in his 1950 book. A movie of the same name, starring Steve McQueen and James Garner, was made in 1963. Hitler ordered the execution of fifty Allied airmen who were re-captured after escaping from this camp.

very sick, which the Russians found hilarious. After two action-filled days, we were fortunate, very fortunate, to pass through a village where a small advance unit of the U.S. Army was just on the point of following orders to pull back to the west. We said good-bye to our Russian friends and proceeded to the U.S. base at Halle with the advance unit.

The U.S. Airforce flew us to Brussels, Belgium, on May 7, 1945. I don't remember anything about VE Day, but I was told I had a good time. The next day, the RAF flew us back to England.

The RAF did not want to demobilize us too fast and offered us POW Rehabilitation. I got posted to a rehab centre in Scarborough. There, I got a job with a consulting engineer, working on municipal engineering. The company got my services for free, as I was still paid by the RAF, a very good deal all round. I enjoyed the work and benefited from the experience professionally. I became an expert designer for sewage disposal works. Some said I had found my proper place in the s—t.

About August 1946, I got word that I was assigned to a ship to Canada. In September, I got demobilized, resigned my job, packed up, and sailed from Liverpool on September 28 aboard the *Scythia*, along with several hundred war brides of Canadian servicemen. I arrived in Winnipeg, via the CPR about the ninth of October, a Friday, and I literally didn't have two nickels in my pocket. I went out on Saturday, and in the afternoon, landed a job at Vulcan Ironworks as a draftsman.

Some of the Anson trainees and staff at No. 33 SFTS.
(Photo: Commonwealth Air Training Plan Museum)

Fortunately, at Stalag Luft 3, there was a good educational program set up, which was supported by educational establishments in the U.K. I enrolled and applied to take the final exam of the Institution of Structural Engineers while I was in prison camp, but because of the Russian advance, I didn't know how I made out.

I did pass and became a chartered structural engineer. This was sufficient to qualify me to join the Association of Professional Engineers and to be licensed to practise in Manitoba.

By December 1946, I had a job offer from CN Rail. I worked there, designing bridges and inspecting them all over Western Canada, from Long Lac, Ontario, to Vancouver Island, and from Churchill, Manitoba, to Duluth, Minnesota. In 1968, I became the head regional engineer for western Canada of bridges and structures.

My wartime marriage ended in divorce in 1966. Viviane, my second wife, and I were married in 1971, but sadly, she died of cancer some years later. In 1992, I was very fortunate to gain the friendship of a very wonderful lady, who finally gave in to my demands to marry me. Dorothy Kozar was a widow with two sons.

May 2005

Note: One of those sons is my husband, Verne. The Kozar family will be forever grateful to Bill for his devotion to Dorothy, who now resides at a seniors' residence in Winnipeg. They had twelve wonderful years together. Bill loved Canada and, because of his job, had seen far more of our wilderness areas than most Canadians can ever hope to. His legacy can be seen in the bridges and structures he designed and inspected for the CNR throughout Western Canada

ERIC (DUSTY) TITHERIDGE

WINNIPEG, MANITOBA

It is probably important for the reader to realize that this story is being written more than sixty years after the major players appeared on the scene. Also, it should be understood that the whole affair must be viewed with World War II in the background. Nowadays, an overseas assignment of six months is maximum. I was overseas for three-and-a-half years and served in sixty-one different locations, some for only a few weeks, and the longest almost one year. The performance of the post office during those war years was quite remarkable.

When the war broke out in 1939, I had just completed high school, and I was sixteen years old. Because my home was near the south coast of England, I witnessed some of the dogfights between the RAF and the Luftwaffe over the English Channel during the Battle of Britain. I stayed with an aunt in London during the Blitz. The evacuation of Dunkirk filled the newspapers.

The Germans had taken Poland, swarmed through the Netherlands and Belgium, and practically all French resistance had been wiped out prior to 1941. Britain faced an animated Germany alone, and the threat of invasion was very real. The U.K. was placed on a strict war footing as soon as war was declared. Food and most other necessities were severely rationed. Being an island, all goods had to be imported by sea. There was little room for luxuries.

The feats performed by the RAF during the Battle of Britain, amplified by Winston Churchill's oratory, attracted many young men. When I was eighteen, I immediately volunteered to serve. Luckily, being physically fit, I was accepted for aircrew training. So I took the king's shilling and began my RAF career from the Lord's Cricket Ground in London. With the rank of AC2, I completed my initial training at Stratford-upon-Avon and

Dusty and Ruth Titheridge on their wedding day.
(Photo: Titheridge Family)

moved to No. 6 EFTS at Sywell, Northamptonshire, as an LAC. There, I undertook my first flight in a Tiger Moth. That was a very thrilling experience, and one that I still remember vividly. I was hooked!

By early 1942, I was on my way to North America. The United States had allowed a small number of RAF cadets to learn to fly from its civilian training schools prior to its declaration of war in December 1941 when the Japanese bombed Pearl Harbor.

There was a dramatic change from the U.K. to New York. Instead of a rigidly enforced blackout every night, that city was vibrantly alive. The dazzling lights on Broadway and the tall skyscrapers were most impressive for a newcomer from Europe. There was no shortage of anything! From the $10 we were allowed to draw from our meagre pay to tour the Big Apple, I spent the first two on a banana split. My limited funds were soon exhausted. My aspiration to reach the top of the Empire State Building was never achieved.

The next stop was in Albany, Georgia, where we were taught how the Americans won their war of independence. We had an introduction to U.S. Army drill, and the khaki-coloured uniform I wore was an added attraction. I was selected to go to Tuscaloosa, Alabama, to train. Although I completed my first solo flight in a P17 Stearman within the ten-hour time limit, I was considered unsuitable for further pilot training and was ordered to pack my kit for travel to Trenton, Ontario.

One of Canada's greatest contributions to the war effort was the British Commonwealth Air Training Plan. It was growing rapidly and was producing many aircrew tradesmen, other than pilots. Brandon, Manitoba, was one of the major manning depots, and although I had requested a posting to Edmonton, the draft to that destination had been filled before the letter "T" for Titheridge had been reached. So, I ended up in Brandon.

There wasn't much to do in the Wheat City, and when I had the opportunity to get a forty-eight-hour pass to leave the camp, I seized it and boarded a bus to the national park at Clear Lake. This was the summer of 1942. An eclipse of the moon had been forecast for that evening, and I walked to the pier on the lakefront for a better view. There were three lovely girls on the pier that evening, presumably with the same object in mind. One of them was Ruth, who was camping with her sister and a friend. I was thunderstruck and delighted to be able to spend the whole next day in Ruth's company. We walked, rode bicycles, and talked at length. I discovered that she had just graduated with her arts degree from Brandon College and was in training to become a lab technician at the local hospital. She was just twenty-one and had voted for the first time. What a put down! I was nineteen and still ineligible.

Before there were any other developments in my love life, I was posted to Winnipeg, and I spent the next four months undergoing an air navigator's course at No. 5 Air Observer School. We exchanged a few letters during this time, and although Ruth had another boyfriend, I did get an invitation to visit with her family in Brandon for Christmas 1942. Shortly after, I spent a leave in Chicago before my next posting to Moncton, New Brunswick. Within a few days, I was in New York where I boarded the *Queen Elizabeth* en route to England.

My rank had gone from AC2, to LAC, to sergeant, and then to pilot officer! It took a few more months before I ended up in an OTU, and began serious training on Wellingtons for a career in Bomber Command. We formed a crew which consisted of an Australian pilot, an Australian wireless operator, a British navigator, a British bomb aimer, and a British rear gunner.

We were initiated into active bombing experience with a flight to a target in France. Suddenly, there was a need for more crews in North Africa. However, instead of flying a new aeroplane out to that war zone, we found ourselves on board an old French ship heading for Algeria. We arrived in Phillipville and then rode the colonial French railway system to Tunis, the capital of Tunisia. We joined 150 Squadron RAF, then based in Kairouan, a Sahara Desert oasis. The airplanes were antiquated Wellingtons. Tents provided our living quarters and sand abounded. The food was awful!

As the Allied forces overcame the German Afrika Korps from both east and west, we were able to move north to assist in the capture of Sicily. We then moved into southern Italy just before Christmas 1943. From Foggia, Italy, we attacked targets all over southern Europe, with particular emphasis on the River Danube's heavy rail and barge traffic. Most of the German oil supply originated in the Ploesti region of Romania. It moved from there by rail tank car or river barge. The larger cities on the river were important factory sites and, therefore, bombing targets.

Throughout this period, I was keeping a continuous connection with Ruth via mail. Indeed, I used to trade my beer and cigarette ration for air letter forms so that I could write more frequently. She responded in kind.

I survived my tour of operational flying and left Italy for Palestine in June 1944. I became a navigation instructor at a Middle East OTU for about a year, by which time the war in Europe ended. My next job was in Mersa Matruh, Egypt, where I monitored the transfer of military personnel across the Mediterranean.

At this point, I was carefully contemplating what I should do with my life after my discharge from the RAF. My relationship with Ruth was deepening, and I think we openly declared our affection for one another by mail while I was in that desert outpost. I had no trouble at all making my decision to emigrate to Canada, although I knew it would be hard for my parents to take. I applied for entry to the University of Manitoba from Cairo, Egypt, and was accepted. All I had to do was get there! That wouldn't be easy.

Transatlantic sea travel was difficult, and air travel was impossible. Finally, I received permission to enter Canada as a landed immigrant. A fortuitous encounter with another potential immigrant led to an opportunity to sign on as a cabin boy on a tramp steamer out of Leith, Scotland. It took fourteen days to cross the ocean. I landed in Montreal, caught the next train to Winnipeg, and Ruth met me at the CPR station. We exchanged out first kiss, and before the weekend was over, we were engaged to be married!

I began classes at the University of Manitoba the next day. Our wedding took place in Brandon on May 3, 1947. We have been blessed with four wonderful children and remain steadfastly in love sixty-three years after we first met at Clear Lake during the eclipse of the moon.

October 2005

KEITH MUNSON VOLLER

OTTAWA, ONTARIO

I grew up in Frensham, a lovely English village in Surrey. It is quite well known for its small lakes called Big Pond and Little Pond. St. Mary's, the 750-year-old church with its witches' cauldron, was the centre of most of the villagers' activities. The trips to the seaside made it the most ideal spot for a boy to grow up. Because we had gardens for fresh vegetables, pheasants, rabbits, and free-range eggs from the surrounding estates, we didn't fare too badly during the thirties.

Two of my chums and I joined the air cadets until we were old enough to join the regular forces. The eldest, Eddie Brunham, received a call from the RAF to take his medical at Reading. I took the day off and went also. Once at the recruiting office, I decided to sign on for the Royal Navy at the age of seventeen, and I was called up in January 1943. I finished basic training at HMS *Collingwood* and then volunteered to serve on submarines. I had an uncle who served on K class submarines in World War I, and I was influenced by his stories. The Service was a very important tradition in my family. My father served with the East Surrey Regiment; my brother was a member of the Life Guards; one brother-in-law served with the 9th Lancers and

Keith and Joan Voller (in uniform) during their courtship.
(Photo: Voller Family)

another with the Royal Navy.

I did my submarine training at HMS *Dolphin*, and then I had a short trip aboard H 28. After that, I was drafted to a lend-lease American submarine, the P 512. It was used to train the Canadian navy in anti-submarine attacks off the coast of Bermuda. I was fortunate to be based at St. George in beautiful Bermuda for seven or eight months.

After my Bermuda posting, I was transferred to the HMS *Sportsman*, but because it was being re-fitted in the naval yard in Philadelphia, I was sent to the submarine, L 23, which was docked at Digby, Nova

Keith and Joan Voller on their wedding day.
(Photo: Voller Family)

Scotia, instead of enjoying the good life in Philadelphia. The L 23 had been built in 1917 and was used as a decoy to train RCN personnel in anti-submarine warfare.

One day, while I was doing my laundry in a bucket on the sub casing in Digby, two Canadian WREN in the Women's Royal Canadian Naval Service walked down to the jetty and asked if they could have a tour of the sub. I took them below where there was no shortage of tour guides for these attractive servicewomen in their neat uniforms, and I returned to my chores. The girls were certainly a big hit with the sailors. One WREN had red hair and was slim and neat, while the other one had dark hair and big brown eyes. After the tour, we talked, and one thing led to another. We agreed to meet on the WRENs' next off-duty day.

The next week, the red-haired WREN, Joan Amy Thompson, made her appearance, and my life was never the same again. We went to the one movie show in Digby, had a meal at the Cornwallis Café and agreed to meet again, which we did, again and again. Our favorite song from those days was "It Had to Be You." We became engaged before I was sent back to the *Sportsman* in Philadelphia.

After my time on the *Sportsman*, I was very fortunate to be drafted to a new S- class sub, the *Sentinel*. How great it was to have up-to-date radar and asdic [submarine detector] to operate. After running up trials, the new sub was called for service in the Far East. After two months, the posting was cancelled because the end of the war with Japan was in sight, and we were no longer needed.

After the war ended, Joan was allowed to travel to the U.K. in order to take her discharge at HMCS *Niobe* in London. She made this request so that we could be married in England. We had a naval wedding at St. Mary's Church in Frensham on April 20, 1946, over sixty years ago. After the marriage, I still had six months to serve in the Royal Navy before my discharge. After I left the Service, we moved to Sheffield, Yorkshire, where both of Joan's parents were born and bred. Many of her relatives still lived there. I joined the Sheffied City Police Force after training at Cannock near Birmingham. I enjoyed being a bobby.

Our first daughter, Susan Clarissa, was born a year later in May. About this time, Joan felt the first pangs of homesickness. Consequently, I resigned from the police force, and after tearful good-byes in Sheffield and Frensham, we sailed aboard the *Aquitania* in October 1947. We arrived in Halifax and went by train to Joan's home in Ottawa. A second daughter, Mary Kathryn Louise, was born in 1948; a son, William David, made his appearance in 1952. We also have three grown grandchildren.

I became a Canadian citizen in the early fifties when I was employed by the National Research Council. I served as president of the Research Council Employees' Association for many years before retirement. I'm a member of the Ottawa Submariners' Association which has many members.

My secrets of our long and happy marriage are: (1) recognizing very early who was the boss, and (2) never falling out of love with the slim redhead of long ago.

July 2006

John Watson

AURORA, ONTARIO

My husband, John Watson, was born in Blackpool, England. After he joined the RAF, he was posted to Carberry, Manitoba, to learn to fly. When the airmen from Carberry spent their leaves in Winnipeg, many families offered to billet them. My parents wanted to do their part, too, and opened up their home in St. Vital [suburb in Winnipeg] to the boys on leave. Some of the fellows we billeted would fly over my parents' house, which was easily identifiable from the air as it was on a bend of the Red River, and they would waggle their wings to let us know they were coming. I remember when one plane flew under the Elm Park Bridge, and it made quite a splash in the newspaper. I don't know if it was one of our fellows or not. They didn't say.

My family shared a lodge at George Lake [near Point du Bois] with friends, and we often took the young British airmen there. The Canadian camp experience had a huge influence on their impressions of Canada. The space, privacy and freedom to fish, swim, and laze around were very important to all the young Brits, and they talked about it for years after. They regarded it as their safe place during their training years, and it helped to make their time in Canada special.

One of our regulars spent every second weekend with us and, one time, he brought John along. We clicked right from the start, and we began dating. After John finished his flying course, he was kept back as an instructor, but as luck would have it, he was posted to Estevan, Saskatchewan. He was still close enough to Winnipeg to spend his leaves at my home. John enjoyed his time in the small towns where he was posted, and he was treated very well by the local people, but he preferred to be in Winnipeg. Maybe I had

John and Pat Watson on their wedding day.
(Photo: Watson Family)

something to do with that. John enjoyed his time in Canada, and the winters never seemed to bother him, although he never dressed properly for it. As I recall, none of the airmen did.

In 1944, the war was winding down and not as many pilots were needed. The base where John was instructing was closing down, and he was scheduled to return to Britain. Before he left, he wanted to be sure no one else would claim me while he was gone, and we became engaged. John and his friend, Johnny Slocombe, who was engaged to my cousin, went to Birks Jewellers together and bought engagement rings. Johnny took Shirley back to England where they farmed, raising pigs, fowl and cattle. Shirley died about 1990, but Johnny is still in Sussex.

John wanted me to go to Britain, so that we could be married there. I applied to go, but I had to wait until passage was available. In February 1945, I received a notice stating that I had to be ready to leave within twenty-four hours. I didn't hesitate for a second, but my mother was devastated, and there were lots of tears at the train station. I boarded an old banana boat in Halifax, and it wasn't the most comfortable ship in the world. I was seasick for the first few hours but, afterwards, I was fine.

I managed to make the train connections to Blackpool where John's family lived, and they were wonderful to me. My parents sent over many care packages containing soap, flour, lard, cooking oil, dried fruit and nuts—items that were rationed in Britain, but still available in Canada. It made all the difference to our baking. John's family was very grateful for these luxuries.

Our wedding was held in a beautiful old Anglican church, and our reception was modest due to wartime conditions and rationing. John flew a Mosquito bomber

Christmas leave in Carberry, Manitoba 1940: British airmen, having just arrived from the U.K., celebrate Christmas away from home with a local family.
(Photo: Carberry Plains Archives)

175

The YWCA Hostess House was a popular destination at No. 33 SFTS.
(Photo: Commonwealth Air Training Plan Museum)

over occupied territory at night. He was stationed at various bases in England, but he also spent time in Malta and Egypt with Squadron 163B. I met John's navigator when he came to our wedding. John never talked much about his flying operations, but I could tell they weren't fun. I could hear the planes leaving, and I never slept until I heard them returning early in the morning.

Our daughter was born at the home of my in-laws. In all, I spent about two years in England. They were interesting, busy, and challenging times, but I was in love, and took each day as it came. I followed John from base to base and tried my best to make a good home for him and the baby. I didn't worry about much else except the day-to-day details of living in wartime Britain.

My parents kept pressuring us to return to Canada after the war, and John finally agreed in 1947. John had worked in a bank before the war, and my father was able to get him a job at the Imperial Bank. It was very comforting for John to know that he had a job waiting for him in Canada. He never regretted his decision because he knew he would have a better life here. John always referred to himself as a war bride, much to the amusement of the family.

John and I had six children, five of them girls. Four years ago, we moved to Aurora to be closer to our son, and although we missed our friends in Winnipeg, we made new friends here. John had surgery in October 2004, but he didn't survive the operation, and I miss him terribly. I live in my own private apartment in the lower part of my son's house. Many grandchildren and great-grandchildren continue to make my life interesting.

Pat Watson, September 2006

WILLIAM (BILL) WEBSTER

LONDON, ONTARIO

I was born at South Molton, Devon, but my family later moved to Brighton where I grew up. I joined the RAF on March 26, 1939, my eighteenth birthday, and was posted to No. 48 Squadron in Kent. There, I was part of No. 1 School of Air Navigation. The school was moved to St. Athens in Wales because it was thought it would be safer for training. After being bombed by the Germans in that location, too, it was decided to move the school, complete with aircraft, out of the country.

In November 1940, we boarded the *Duchess of Richmond*, although we didn't know where we were headed. At that stage of the war, U-boats were attacking shipping with great success, and we were on our own, with no escorts. While at sea, the captain told us that we were heading for Canada. On November 5, we saw a convoy passing in the opposite direction, and I took a picture of it from the deck. Later that evening, we heard gunfire and saw flashes. We didn't find out what happened until we docked in Quebec. Apparently, the German battleship, the *Admiral Scheer*, had spotted and intercepted the passing convoy, and the armed merchant ship, the *Jervis Bay*, the only escort, was sunk. This event allowed the convoy to scramble, saving them and us.

The British Commonwealth Air Training Plan was just getting started, and we formed No. 31 Air Navigation School at Port Albert near Goderich, Ontario. I was part of the operational staff and remained there until early 1943 when I returned to the U.K. When we arrived at Port Albert, it had not been completed, and it was just a sea of mud. My first Canadian winter was quite a shock.

I met my wife on a blind date. That's how many of us usually met the girls. One of the fellows would get to know a local girl, and she would always have a friend. In my case, it happened to be Helen Marie Wiles, who worked in a small tea shop which sold the best ice cream in Goderich. When Helen asked me home for supper one night, her mother asked me where I lived in England, and I told her that I was from Brighton. She said, "So am I." Apparently, Helen's mother had lived two streets away from my family home and had gone to school with my father. From then on, I could do no wrong.

Our relationship developed into a romance, and I proposed to Helen in her home. Upon hearing of our engagement, Helen's father said, "If you get married, you make your bed, and you lie in it." Because we were both under twenty-one, we had to get permission from our parents and from my commanding officer. I had to wait to get a return wire from my parents in England giving me official permission. After we received everybody's permission, we were married on January 17, 1942, in Stratford, Ontario, because Helen's parents had moved there from Goderich.

I was posted to the U.K. in early 1943, and my wife wanted to join me there. We made the arrangements, and after she got the call, Helen proceeded to Halifax where she boarded a ship that carried munitions, cheese, and six passengers. It was three weeks before her convoy finally docked, and because of wartime secrecy, I did not know the port or the day of arrival. I sent a letter through the Air Ministry giving Helen instructions to wire my family after she arrived. I told my family to contact me at my station as soon as they heard any news about Helen's arrival. The plan was that I would ask for compassionate leave and would fetch her as soon as I knew where she was. Because she was very independent, Helen decided to leave Liverpool, where the ship docked, and she made her way to Brighton on her own. This meant crossing England through the London blackout and then on to Brighton. My parents and sister had received a cable from the Air Ministry and were able to meet each train from London that night. They notified me, and I was able to get to the station to meet her. My family welcomed Helen with open arms, and my sister, who was about the same age as my wife, was quite happy to have such a good friend.

Within two weeks of her arrival, Helen was called up for war work. All women with no children in the U.K. were conscripted and were expected to help with the war effort in some capacity. Helen's job was sewing up asbestos pads, but she was never told what they were for. The little sewing factory where she worked was located in a hotel on the seafront in Brighton where mines would often be washed up onto the beach. Consequently, the girls working in the hotel would often be evacuated until the beach was cleared.

Back in 1939, I had been trained as an air gunner, and I was also an electrician. When I was not flying, I did the electrical work on the aircraft. In 1944, when I was with No. 233 Squadron, I embarked upon a new phase of my air force career. I received training in glider towing and paratroop transport in order to support Operation Overlord. We boarded our planes on June 5, 1944, the night before D-Day, and towed gliders, filled with paratroopers, to France. Some of the paratroopers that we transported defended the famous Pegasus Bridge in Normandy.[12]

We had other operations of a similar nature, such as the Rhine Crossing and the paratroop drop at Arnhem. Our squadron also transported the wounded back to England as soon as landing strips became available. Finally, we were used in Operation Manna when we dropped food parcels to the starving Dutch people.

After the war was over, I was demobilized. We returned to Canada in 1948 because Helen's mother was quite sick at that time. We settled in London, Ontario. My first job was as an electrician with the CNR, but the shops closed in 1960. Fortunately, I got a position as an electrical technician at Victoria Hospital in London, and I retired as the electrical and bio tech supervisor in 1985.

I have no regrets about moving to Canada. Life has been good to us here, but I still love England. We tried to return every two or three years to the U.K. when we could afford it in order to see my family. On one of these trips, I crossed the English Channel to Normandy, the site of the D-Day Invasion, and visited several sites there.

We have been gifted with a son, a daughter, two grandchildren and two great-grandchildren. Sadly, my wife passed away in the year 2000.

September 2005

---

[12] Major John Howard led the glider assault on Pegasus Bridge. Richard Todd portrayed his experiences in the 1962 movie, *The Longest Day*, which was based on the 1959 book of the same name by Cornelius Ryan.

HENRIK WESENBERG

BATHURST, NEW BRUNSWICK

I recently interviewed Anna Wesenberg, an absolutely delightful lady, who is the widow of a Norwegian Merchant Navy officer. Her niece, Melynda Jarratt, e-mailed this message to me: "The story of how my aunt and uncle met, fell in love and then married is right out of the movies. He was a dashing young officer who wore a white uniform, and he was absolutely gorgeous, especially with that accent. She was a small town girl from Bathurst, New Brunswick. No wonder they fell in love. What makes it interesting is that he kept all the documentation which the family found last year when cleaning out the attic of the house. None of us knew it was there. It was like touching history. There are even top secret documents there. He was the only English-speaking officer on the ship, and he had to translate everything for the captain."

My husband's ship, the *Borgholm*, was docked in Bergen, Norway, when the Germans began to enter Oslo. Norway was occupied by the Germans during the war. To keep the ships out of enemy hands, Haakon VII, King of Norway, ordered all Norwegian ships to leave and to go to Allied ports. Henrik's ship proceeded to England and, for the rest of the war, the *Borgholm* sailed with the Atlantic convoys carrying ammunition and weapons.

The Borgholm happened to be docked at Bathurst, New

Henrik and Anna Wesenberg on their wedding day.
(Photo: Wesenberg Family)

Brunswick, when Henrik broke his wrist in an accident on board the ship. He was sitting in the doctor's office waiting to get his wrist set when he noticed an attractive secretary, and in spite of the pain, he asked her for a date. It just so happened that the doctor's secretary was my sister. She declined because she was engaged to be married, but she mentioned that she had a sister who might be interested. Henrik agreed, and my sister then arranged a blind date for us. I was also a secretary at the time, and I worked at the local paper mill.

Henrik and I clicked right away, and whenever his ship came to Saint John, New Brunswick, he would travel by train to Bathurst in order to see me. The trip took about three hours, and I think he came to see me four times. At the end of the last visit, we both knew that we wanted to get married. Henrik was such a gentleman, quiet and polite, and he completely charmed my family and friends. During our short courtship, we did the usual things dating couples did in those days. We went to dances and movies, and we visited friends. During the time that Henrik was on convoy duty, we exchanged many letters.

Henrik received several citations and medals for his dedication to duty, and one incident stands out in my memory. Henrik's ship was near the mouth of the Humber River in England when German planes attacked. The ship had no armaments to speak of, only two machine guns mounted onto the deck and the bridge. Henrik manned one of the machine guns as the planes strafed the deck. After the first attack, the planes returned and attacked again. He was the second officer on board, and when the first officer was killed, he was promoted to his place. In another incident, Henrik took a German officer prisoner, but I can't recall the circumstances. Since my stroke, my memory is not as good as it once was. It was fortunate that the *Borgholm* was never torpedoed because she usually carried ammunition. One torpedo would have blown the ship up.

After the war ended, Henrik paid for his passage to Canada, and we were married in 1946. When it became known that I was leaving Canada, someone said to me that I wouldn't know anyone in Norway. I told her that I could move to the next town in New Brunswick and not know anybody. My family knew that Henrik was a fine man and that he would make me very happy.

After we were married, we went to New York to try to arrange passage to Norway, but it was next to impossible. Henrik had a friend at the Norwegian consul who helped us with the tickets. The trip was hell on earth. It took twelve days to get to Norway, and I lost twelve pounds during that time. I fed the fishes all the way there. I threw up things I hadn't even eaten. You know what they say when you're seasick: at first, you think you're going to die, and then you're afraid you won't.

We lived in Norway for five years, and our first son was born there. Henrik's family was wonderful to me, and I had the best in-laws anyone could have. It didn't matter to them that I was Roman Catholic and they were Lutheran. Whenever I wanted to go to church, there was always somebody willing to look after my son. Henrik's mother and sister were opera fans, and they got me hooked, too.

I found Norwegian easy to learn, and I still can speak it to this day. At first, Henrik's family spoke English to me, but I insisted that they speak Norwegian so that I would learn. I started off by reading labels on cans and boxes.

What really impressed me about Norway was the fact that the royal family seemed so ordinary. I saw the royal family get on buses, and they even strapped on their skis beside us on the ski hills. At the opera, the royal family sat directly in front of us. I was also impressed by the winters in Norway because they were much milder than in Bathurst. Henrik worked for a shipping company, and my son and I would often accompany him on his trips. I never regretted the time I spent in Norway because I

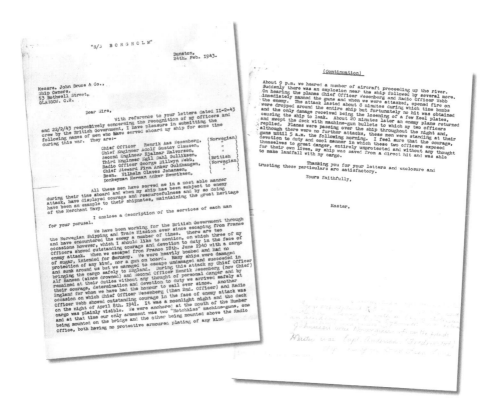

Letter of citation for Henrik Wesenberg.
(Photo: Wesenberg Family)

had some wonderful experiences and met some wonderful people.

This was the time of the Cold War with the Soviet Union. When I saw that the Norwegians were stocking up on matches, canned goods, candles, etc., because of a possible invasion from the Soviet Union, I got cold feet. The Norwegians had been so unprepared before the German invasion during the war that they were taking no chances this time. I talked Henrik into leaving Norway, and we arrived back in Bathurst in 1951. Henrik's family accepted the decision and never tried to change our minds. By that time, I had lost my Canadian citizenship, and we both had to apply as new immigrants.

Fortunately, my parents had a large house in Bathurst, and we lived in separate quarters in part of it. After he arrived in Canada, Henrik took an instrumentation course and got a job looking after the equipment at the paper mill. He enjoyed this job, and he met some good friends there. Henrik enjoyed Canada, but he did miss his family back in Norway.

Canada has been good to us, and our family grew to include five boys and one girl. I have four grandchildren to date. My daughter is in the Canadian Forces and has seen the world. I lost one son in a fire.

Sadly, Henrik died in 1975 at the age of sixty-two. He had always wanted to be buried in Norway beside his parents. Henrik's sister came to Canada and, together, we took his cremated remains back to Norway. In all, I have been back to Norway four times during the years, and some members of Henrik's family have visited me in Bathurst. I have been a widow for over thirty years and have not re-married. No one else could ever replace Henrik. I still miss him.

Anna Wesenberg, February 2006

CLIFFORD (WESTY) WESTGARTH-TAYLOR

BARRIE, ONTARIO

Westy and Leora Westgarth-Taylor
shortly after they were married.
(Photo: Westgarth-Taylor Family)

As a past-president of 441 Wing of the Airforce Association of Canada, I read an advertisement about male war brides that was published in our monthly bulletin. I decided to respond so that I could relate the story of my late husband and myself.

Clifford Westgarth-Taylor was known to his family and friends as "Westy." He was born in Norfolk, County of Cambridge, England, and was attending Cambridge University before he joined the RAF. He was sent to Pensacola, Florida, for pilot training, but washed out because he didn't have the depth perception needed for landing an aircraft. He was then sent to Moncton, New Brunswick, to be trained as a wireless operator / air gunner. They called them "WAGS" at the time. At the end of his training, he was kept back as an officer/instructor and was posted to Malton, Ontario, at No. 1 Air Observer School.

During the war, I served as a civilian flight clerk with No. 1 AOS at Malton. Consequently, because of my position, I was in daily contact with the students and the instructors on the base. I looked after the schedules for aircraft maintenance, refuelling, flights, and other records.

Airmen from many countries trained under the BCATP. One of the persons that I had reason to be in contact with almost daily was Flight Lieutenant Westgarth-Taylor, RAF C151180, and I was attracted to him almost immediately. He was so handsome and so nice, and his accent was wonderful. He used to tease me when I entered the flight room to post the schedules, and I thoroughly enjoyed it.

Westy eventually asked for a date, and we saw each other when we could.

It was difficult because our work schedules often conflicted, but it wasn't long before we became serious. Westy proposed while we were enjoying our after-dinner coffee at a restaurant in Toronto. I didn't get an engagement ring until after my first child was born, however. My engagement ring had belonged to Westy's great-grandmother, and I have treasured it ever since. It was well worth the wait.

Five months after our first date, Westy and I were married, much to the dismay of my parents. My father tried to talk me out of it by saying, "He's in the war, and you know what could happen." I said that I was aware of all that, and told him that I still wanted to marry Westy. Now, I can understand my parents' concern because we were very young. I was nineteen and Westy was twenty-one. Westy had to ask the base commander for permission to get married, but the base commander said that he didn't think he could stop him from getting married anyway. My parents eventually came around, and we were married on August 27, 1943, in Toronto. We don't have any wedding pictures, but it didn't seem to matter at the time.

Two weeks after our wedding, Westy was posted to Penfield Ridge for training on bombers. After he completed the course, he was sent to Doval to await a further posting. Eventually, he was sent to Nassau in the Bahamas with Ferry Command where he served for the rest of the war. Fortunately, because he was in Ferry Command, he was able to spend some of his leaves with me. Westy had one unexpected leave when he was sent home to recuperate from malaria. Needless to say, that as a result of such leaves, we had two sons by the end of the war. During his service, Westy helped to ferry aircraft to various places around the world such as South America, the Azores, and Egypt.

At the end of the war, Westy was sent back to England to be demobilized, and he had to convince the British authorities to return him to Canada to be with his family. They wanted to bring me and the two children to England, but Westy pointed out that it would be cheaper to send him to Canada. He was granted permission and was given passage on a war bride ship. It was quite an experience for him, since there were hundreds of British war brides and their babies on board. After the ship arrived in Halifax, Westy wanted to get off the ship as quickly as possible before all the war brides and their babies disembarked. Naturally, he wanted to avoid all the fuss and commotion associated with small children. As he stepped onto the dock, he was surprised to hear a band serenading him with the familiar tune, "Here Comes the Bride." He never forgot his first welcome to Canada!

Westy had quite a time obtaining work because he was not a Canadian citizen, and was laid off from a job with War Assets. However, he did find a good job with Canadian General Electric in the engineering department and, later, became a product service specialist.

Westy was very community-minded and was active in the Airforce Association, the Legion, Emergency Measures, Boy Scouts, Air Cadets, and the church. He even ran for city council. In addition to our two sons who were born during the war, we adopted a daughter. As time went by, eight grandchildren and one great-grandchild came along.

Westy and I returned to England in 1953 for his brother's wedding, and I met his family for the first time. They were wonderful and were very good to the children and me.

Needless to say, we had a very busy and interesting life, although it ended much too soon. Westy succumbed to a heart attack in 1975 after a very active life in Canada. I am proud to have been the wife of a British war groom.

Leora Westgarth-Taylor, April 2006

RALPH WILD

WINNIPEG, MANITOBA

I was born in Rotherham, Yorkshire, England, in 1918. I joined the RAF in 1938, but my admission was deferred until 1939. At that time, there was conscription, and everyone had to put in six months of service time. War was soon declared, and my six months became seven years. I volunteered for aircrew, but groundcrew were also badly needed. I was selected to be trained in aircraft instrument repair and was sent to various stations in southern England. During the Battle of Britain, I worked on Hurricane fighters at North Weald, Essex. At that time, I was working eighteen to twenty hours a day servicing new aircraft and repairing others. Lady

Ralph and Myrla Wild on their wedding day.
(Photo: Wild Family)

pilots transported the new aircraft from the factories, and we got them ready for battle. We lived and worked under difficult conditions because our fighter station was bombed regularly by the Germans. Our accommodations were destroyed, and we had to live in tents.

When some of the German planes accidentally bombed London, Churchill ordered bombing attacks on Berlin. This action agitated Hitler. He decided to bomb British cities instead of RAF stations, and this change of targets saved Britain. It took the pressure off the fighter stations and gave the RAF time to repair the planes and to train more pilots.

After the Battle of Britain, I volunteered for overseas service, not knowing where I would be sent. I came to Canada on the first RAF draft in December 1940 on the *Louis Pasteur*. We were issued tropical khaki clothing, and we assumed that we were going to Crete. After we got on board, we were told to go to the starboard side of the ship to change into our blues. The switch in uniforms was done to confuse the spies on the dock who might notify U-boats about our destination.

I was destined for an unknown place called Carberry, Manitoba. The train did not go all the way into Carberry, and after we disembarked, we marched two miles to the base in the midst of a Canadian winter. After three winters in Canada, I got used to the climate and didn't think about it much. The base at Carberry was at the beginning stages because the BCATP was just getting started. I stayed in Carberry from December 1940 to August 1943, and I was a corporal in charge of instrument repair for the planes that were used to train pilots.

Soon after our arrival at No. 33 SFTS, we were given a week's leave in Winnipeg, over one hundred miles away. A special train was put on for us, and the Women's Auxiliary met us at the station. We had to call out the city or town where we came from in Britain, and someone in the crowd would claim us. That was the system used to find billets for us. When we got back to Carberry, we were given another week off because the planes and pilots hadn't arrived, and there was nothing to do. We airmen were well-treated by the citizens of Winnipeg and Carberry, and they wouldn't let us pay for anything while we were billeted in their homes. They couldn't do enough for us.

A friend was assigned to my future wife's family, and he brought me to their home in June 1941. This invitation changed my life and determined my future. When Myrla-Ruth Easton and I looked across the dinner table at each other, bells rang! We started to see each other whenever we could and as often as possible. Myrla had just graduated as a nurse and was working at Grace Hospital.

I proposed on March 21, 1943, in the second row from the back in Little Britain Church in Selkirk. I put the ring on Myrla's finger as we sat there. We were married on June 12, 1943, at Home Street United Church in Winnipeg, and we had our honeymoon in Niagara Falls. I didn't want to start a family during wartime, but Myrla did. She said she wanted something to remember me by in case I didn't survive the war, and it was the only thing we ever seriously disagreed about throughout our marriage.

I had promised my mother that I wouldn't marry during wartime, but I didn't keep the promise. Myrla's family liked me, and although they weren't keen on wartime marriages either, they gave us their blessing. The grandmother, however, was a tyrant, and she thought that I probably had three wives back in England.

I often think of one amusing incident that happened after Myrla and I became engaged. Our commanding officer at No. 33 SFTS arranged for dances to be held once or twice a year at the drill hall in Carberry. Arrangements were made to send busloads of young ladies from Winnipeg, Brandon, and other small towns in the area to the dance. It was also customary for airmen to have a forty-eight-hour pass every second week. I arranged for Myrla to come out to one of these dances on the bus from Winnipeg. After the dance, the ladies were escorted back to their buses in order to go back to their original destinations. It transpired that I was on a "48" that weekend, and although I would normally have headed for Winnipeg, I stayed in camp to attend the dance, since my sweetheart was coming to Carberry at my invitation. She would be returning home by chartered bus that evening. Being very much in love, and not wanting to waste the weekend away from her, I talked to the ladies returning to Winnipeg and asked if there was room for me on the bus. Although the bus was reserved for ladies only, I received full co-operation. I sneaked on, stretched out flat on the floor under the rear seat, and the ladies put their legs on top of me. When the military police came on board to check for stowaways, I was not noticed, and I safely made the trip back to the city. Late Sunday evening, I returned on the usual "Airmen's Special" train to Carberry.

On August 1, 1943, my request to re-muster for aircrew finally came through, and I was sent to Regina to train as a navigator. I was there for three months, and then I was posted to No. 5 Navigation School in Winnipeg. I graduated at the top of the class and was commissioned. In March of 1944, I left for England to join Bomber Command.

I was crewed up at the operational training unit in Lossiemouth, Scotland. The RAF had a wonderful system for crewing up. They put you in a room full of airmen and let you find your own crew. The pilot usually picked the navigator, and it went on from there. I was very fortunate because there was a flight lieutenant in my hut who had been trained in Georgia, U.S.A., and had been kept back as an instructor. He was the best pilot anyone could have. He and I were about the same age, twenty-six or so, and most of the other aircrew were younger, about eighteen or nineteen. He and I clicked right away. For our final exam, our crew had a five-hour flight in heavy fog, and we never saw the ground once.

We were posted to No. 10 Squadron at Melbourne, Yorkshire, on Halifax IIIs, and we flew nineteen operations before the war ended. We were lucky and received only a few holes from shrapnel on operations. We were in what was called a VIP squadron. We had excellent equipment that could detect fighters, but we still had to contend with flak.

There were two kinds of flak. The first kind was when the Germans threw everything up at us, including the kitchen sink, and we flew through it. The other kind was called predicted flak, controlled entirely by radar. The German gunners took into account our height and speed, and then aimed at us. We could always tell predicted flak because we could see the five puffs in a row. Someone in the crew would shout, "Predicted flak!" and then the pilot would put the plane into a roll, as the flak would hit us only if we kept flying straight and level. I hated predicted flak because of the G-force that resulted. Everything would float off my desk and I couldn't do anything about it because I couldn't move.

Those of us in the forces appreciated the support we received from the British people during the war, and I have a story that exemplifies this. When I was stationed at Melbourne, Yorkshire, in 1944–45, we had a one-week stand-down every six weeks to recuperate. My family lived about thirty miles away in Rotherham, and I took the opportunity to go home each time. The nearest train station to the camp was at York, a distance of about fifteen miles, and I used my bicycle to get there. All fast trains going south to London and other cities never stopped at Rotherham. This situation presented a problem that I was able to solve. I checked my bike at the baggage storage for one week. I bought my ticket, sought out the guard at the rear of the train and explained my problem. I asked if it was possible for the train to slow down while going through Rotherham station in order to let me jump out. We both went to talk to the engineer, and he agreed to co-operate. When we got within

The RAF Band, performing at one of the dances
at No. 33 SFTS in Carberry, Manitoba.
(Photo: Commonwealth Air Training Plan Museum)

The airmen from No. 33 SFTS will remember the old train station at Carberry.
(Photo: Commonwealth Air Training Plan Museum)

a few miles north of Rotherham, the engineer would sound the horn and slow down almost to a stop. I would jump out and slam the carriage door. The engineer, who had been looking out of his cab, would wave, sound the horn, and continue on. I was never refused this courtesy. In fact, many engineers brought the train to a stop to make sure that I alighted safely. Many engineers at York came out of their cabs to shake my hand. They told me how much they appreciated what I was doing for the war effort, and that it was a pleasure to be of service.

After the European War ended in May 1945, the squadron was posted to Transport Command. We were to fly transport planes in Burma to supply the troops, but I had to take a conversion course first because the navigation on those planes was different. Then, the war with Japan ended, and I didn't get to go to Burma.

My wife and son had come over to Britain during the war in a convoy. Myrla's family was devastated, of course, and they thought they would never see their daughter again. The captain of her ship became ill during the trip, and because my wife was a registered nurse, she was asked to look after him. She was given a special berth near the captain's quarters, which was better than being down in the hold. Because of secrecy during the war, I didn't know when or where she would be arriving. My commanding officer had a friend who was an admiral, and he contacted him on my behalf. The admiral told me, without being direct, that if I were at the Liverpool dock at such and such a time, I might find a surprise. I was given passes to the dock, and I met my wife and son there.

My crew still kept in touch after the war. Aircrew become very close, as everyone depends on everybody else for survival. If one's rear gunner doesn't shoot down an enemy fighter, it doesn't matter how good a pilot or navigator one is. Over the years, members of my crew have visited me in Winnipeg on numerous occasions, and I have visited them in England. Only my pilot and wireless operator are still alive.

After I was demobilized, I went to university, and after graduation, I got a job with the health department in my hometown, Rotherham. My wife was homesick and didn't like the English climate. Life was difficult because rationing was still going on, and we were living with my mother. We came to Canada in 1950. It was the best decision I ever made. I have always felt that Winnipeg is the best place to live.

After we had been established in Winnipeg, we opened up our home to the NATO boys from abroad who were training here. I remembered how well I had been treated during the war, and I wanted to do something for others. One of the boys from England spent almost every weekend with us until he graduated as a navigator, and he became my best friend.

After I arrived in Canada, I got a job with an insurance company, became the claims manager, and retired after thirty years. We have three children, five grandchildren, and one great-grandchild. Sadly, my wife died of cancer in 2000. We had been married for fifty-seven wonderful years.

October 2005

GLOSSARY

ack-ack	anti-aircraft fire
AC2	Aircraftsman Second Class (lowest rank in the Air Force)
Avro Anson	training aircraft
Battle of Britain	aerial conflict between British and German air forces over England in the summer and fall of 1940; Hitler wanted air supremacy before his planned invasion
BCATP	British Commonwealth Air Training Plan
blackout	air-raid defensive precaution; no lights could been seen outside of buildings at night
Blitz	sustained bombing of the U.K. by the German Luftwaffe, September 1940 to May 1941
Bomber Command	branch of the RAF responsible for all bombing activities
British Expeditionary Forces	British forces in Europe during 1939–40
CO	Commanding Officer
Coastal Command	branch of the RAF that defended the U.K. from attacks from the sea (U-boats, etc.)
commissioned	to become an officer
corvette	ship used to protect Atlantic convoys
demobilization	leaving the Service and returning to civilian life
dogfights	close aerial combat between opposing air forces
Dunkirk	port in northern France through which thousands of soldiers from the British Expeditionary Force and the French army were evacuated

EFTS	Elementary Flying Training School
feathered	turning the blades of a propeller in order to reduce air resistance
Ferry Command	branch of the RAF established early in WWII to improve aircraft delivery
Fighter Command	branch of the RAF comprised of fighter aircraft
flak	anti-aircraft fire
Harvard	single-engine, training aircraft
Home Guard	organization of unpaid volunteers whose task was to help repel the anticipated invasion of the U.K.
HQ	headquarters
LAC	Leading Aircraftsman
Lend-lease	planes, ships, and other equipment loaned to Britain by the U.S.
Luftwaffe	German air force
Mark	upgraded model or newer version (often used when referring to Spitfires)
Mess	military term for dining room
OC	Officer Commanding
Operation Overlord	Normandy Invasion
OTU	Operational Training Unit
POW	prisoner of war
RAAF	Royal Australian Air Force
RAF	Royal Air Force (Great Britain)
RCAF	Royal Canadian Air Force
RCN	Royal Canadian Navy

RNZAF	Royal New Zealand Air Force
snafu	situation normal, all fouled up (servicemen often used a more colourful "f" word); glitch
squadron	small unit
SFTS	Service Flying Training School
shrapnel	splinters from an exploding shell
Third Reich	Nazi Germany
Tiger Moth	single-engine, open cockpit biplane used for training purposes
Training Command	branch of the RAF responsible for training personnel
Transport Command	branch of the RAF that transported personnel, equipment, supplies, food, etc.
U-boats	German submarines
VE Day	Victory in Europe Day (official end of the European War)
VJ Day	Victory in Japan Day (official end of the Pacific War)
V1	unmanned flying bomb launched by the Germans
V2	early ballistic missile launched by the Germans
washed out	term used when trainees fail to meet expectations
Wings Parade	graduation ceremony
WOP/AG	Wireless operator / air gunner

Besides the Tiger Moth, the Avro Anson, and the Harvard, the following terms were also used to refer to aircraft: Avro Manchester, Bolingbroke, B-24, Cessna Crane, C-47, Chipmunk, DC-3, Cornell, Dakota, Halifax, Hawker Typhoon, Hurricane, Lockheed Hudson, Lancaster, Liberator, Lysander, Martinet, Maurader, Miles Masters, Mitchell Bomber, Mosquito, Norseman, Oxford, Spitfire, Stearman, Stirling, Ventura, and Vickers Wellington.

Bibliography

Barris, Ted. *Behind the Glory*. Toronto: Macmillan Canada, 1992.

Brickhill, Paul. *The Dam Busters*. London, England: Pan Books, 1983.

Brickhill, Paul. *The Great Escape*. London, England: Cassell & Co., 1988.

Dunmore, Spencer. *Wings for Victory: The Remarkable Story of the British Commonwealth Air Training Plan in Canada*. Toronto: McClelland & Stewart Ltd., 1994.

Granfield, Linda. *Brass Buttons and Silver Horseshoes: Stories from Canada's British War Brides*. Toronto: McClelland & Stewart Ltd., 2002.

Hatch, F.J. *Aerodrome of Democracy: Canada and the British Commonwealth Air Training Plan, 1939–1945*. Ottawa: Canadian Government Publishing Centre, 1983.

Kellow, Bob. *Paths to Freedom*. Winnipeg: Kellow Corporation, 1992.

McDonald, Kenneth. *A Wind on the Heath*. Belleville, Ontario: Epic Press, 2003.

Metcalfe, Robert W. *No Time for Dreams: A Soldier's Six-Year Journey Through WWII*. Burnstown, Ontario: General Store Publishing House, 1997.

Williams, James N. *The Plan: Memories of the British Commonwealth Air Training Plan*. Stittsville, Ontario: John Deyell Company, 1984.

About the Author

Judy Kozar is a recently retired teacher-librarian. She and her husband, Verne, also a retired teacher, enjoy life in Winnipeg, Manitoba. They have two grown daughters, Tracy and Karen.

To order more copies of

Contact:

General Store Publishing House
499 O'Brien Road, Box 415
Renfrew, ON Canada
K7V 4A6

1.800.465.6072
Fax: (613) 432-7184

www.gsph.com

VISA and MASTERCARD accepted